MANY
MANY MANY
GODS
❀ *of* ❀
HINDUISM

*Turning believers into non-believers and
non-believers into believers*

by
SWAMI ACHUTHANANDA

The author can be contacted at swamia@mmmgh.com

ISBN: 1481825526
ISBN-13: 9781481825528

LCCN: 2012924299
CreateSpace Independent Publishing Platform,
North Charleston, SC

In memory of my mother...

Table of Contents

Concepts 65

Controversies **135**

Dear Reader,

Lately I've noticed that you and I are both so busy attending to ourselves that we hardly have time for anything else. The whole world seems to be drifting into an inescapable spiritual vacuum without asking important questions about who we are and why we are here on this planet.

Although the timeless truths of the universe were revealed to us more than five thousand years ago, we no longer have the time to seek answers to the questions of life. Advancements in science were expected to bring us closer to the truth; instead, science has set us farther apart. Unless we are prepared to learn from history, we are bound to make the same mistakes over and over again.

It is always interesting, sometimes revealing, and occasionally enlightening to learn about the truths discovered by the sages of ancient India. The truths are not apparent at once, for the passage of time has distorted them so much that they are often shrouded in myths, lore, and legends.

Many thousands of years ago, a wise sage was illumined. To convey his thoughts, he resorts to metaphors unique to his time and place. Those who write down his words and pass them to history are hardly illumined as the sage, and they misrepresent the metaphor, turning divine truth on its head. You see, it's not hard to imagine how an original idea can become distorted or misunderstood as it moves from place to place and from time to time.

The sacred literature of Hinduism is vast and represents thousands of years of accumulated spiritual experiences, yet it remains largely ignored or forgotten. And that's why I am writing to you. If you agree to stop to think about yourself and your future for a mere ten minutes a day, I will share with you the timeless truths of ancient India. In these moments, you will discover the wisdom of our ancestors and the keys to your future. Well, that's just a few minutes more than the time people would have spent investing in themselves. Like you, the world is too busy to learn the lessons of life.

Swami Achuthananda

CULTURE

In India, the religion is the culture and the culture is the religion.
You cannot learn one without understanding the other.
— Swami Achuthananda

1

What Goes Around Comes Around

As a young kid, I stumbled upon an ancient piece of writing from a little-known Hindu guru. What caught my attention were these lines: "Lend me your full ear, for the thing I am about to tell you is central in becoming a good Hindu. I wish to share with you the truth that is as plain as the day and old as the hills yet ignored in the daily wake of life. Hold on to the next five pivotal words which, if kept closely in your heart, will transform your life from a mere existence into lasting peace and happiness."

The edges were frayed, and the ink had faded, making reading extremely difficult. Holding the manuscript delicately, I peered to the bottom of the page.

"What goes around comes around."

And that was the end. I wish he had written more, for the words made little impact on a nine-year-old boy. The old Swamiji was definitely right, but this was one of the timeless truths I was forced to learn the hard way. Cynicism and skepticism had let me down all these years.

The law of karma states that your thoughts, words, and actions—good and bad—circle back to determine your future. Simply put, you are responsible for your own actions. If you plant goodness, you will reap goodness, but if you plant evil, it will come back and hurt you. It is the universal principle of cause and effect. Later, when life taught me every action has an equal and opposite reaction, the forgotten words of Swamiji reverberated resoundingly in my mind. Evil deeds, like chickens, will sooner or later come home to roost.

Although most people accept this as common sense, others will say, "It is not the fruit of your action, but the gods in heaven that decide your destiny in fate." And the ones immersed in science will claim, "Nonsense! Everything is happenstance, except the laws of science."

While they have difficulty buying into the notion of karma, I am busy booking tickets for a Bollywood thriller. This upsets a handful of people, who are unconvinced by reincarnations or remakes of the past. Most folks, however, appreciate the alluring dances and the melodrama of Indian movies. When the lover rescues his beloved from the clutches of a villain, justice prevails once again in this world. It's sweet karma revisited in cinema.

If you believe the law of karma acts independently to create a fair, self-governing system of justice, then meet me at the gate for an evening of entertainment. We will first dance to the Bollywood beat, and then we will take over the world.

2

The Many Faces of Hinduism

In the poem "The Blind Men and the Elephant," American poet John Godfrey Saxe (1816–1887) relates the fable of six men of Indostan who went to see an elephant, though all of them were blind.

Those who haven't read the poem will learn that the first blind man felt the broad side of the elephant and thought the elephant "to be very like a wall." The second, feeling the tusk, cried out, "No, the elephant is like a spear." Holding the squirming trunk with both hands, the third said, "You are both wrong. The elephant is like a snake." The fourth blind man, feeling the elephant's knee, declared, "Fools, the elephant is clearly like a tree." Caressing the ear, the fifth said, "Did you say tree? The elephant resembles most like a fan." Surprised at all these, the sixth man, seizing the swinging tail, said, "Are you all crazy? Anyone can see the elephant is like a rope."

Like the blind men, people have formed their own perspective on Hinduism from their experience. While some say it is a mystic religion with endless contradictions, others declare Hinduism is about karma and cycles of reincarnation. "Hinduism has millions of gods, many with multiple limbs."

Although each perspective tells us a bit about Hinduism, not one adequately describes the religion. The oldest of the major religions, Hinduism is a collection of traditions, beliefs, and practices deeply rooted in the Indian subcontinent. Many religious movements have led to the present form of Hinduism, but its ancient roots can be traced to the cultures of the Indus Valley and Indo-European people. Many people find Hinduism mystic, for it does not have a historical founder or an authoritative scripture, like the Bible or the Koran.

I tell you this story because to embrace Hinduism you have to understand the Indian culture. When you start observing age-old Hindu practices, you will be struck by the centrality of religion in everyday life displayed through the colors, sounds, and smells of daily rituals. India, the birthplace of Hinduism, is also the land where major Eastern religions like Buddhism, Jainism, and Sikhism were born. It is the largest democratic country, and Hinduism is the third-largest religion in the world. Saxe's fabled country in this poem was of course India.

When you understand enough of the culture, you will meet people not with a handshake but with a Namaste, the traditional Indian greeting. Yoga will cease to exist as a fitness regime anymore, for it will become a means to integrate the body, mind, and soul with god. You will see nature from a different perspective, for every tree, river, and mountain is revered in Hinduism and has a distinct place in its world. You will realize that the many, many, many multi-limbed gods were all manifestations of the one, all-prevailing Brahman.

Are you ready to see the elephant through the jungles of Indian culture? If you are patient, you will see enough of the elephant to finally make sense of Hinduism. And then you'll have something to say worth listening.

> India is the cradle of the human race, the birthplace of human speech, the mother of history, the grandmother of legend, and the great grandmother of tradition. Our most valuable and most instructive materials in the history of man are treasured up in India only.
>
> – Mark Twain (1835–1910)

3

The Banyan Tree

For the first time in history, on July 12, 2007, a Hindu hymn was used to mark the opening session of the US Senate. A handful of conservatives condemned the occasion, saying the prayer flies in the face of the American motto of "One Nation Under God."

"In Hindu, you have not one God, but many, many, many, many, many gods," said David Barton, a religious, right-wing historian. "[This] is not a religion that has produced great things in the world." Soon his supporters joined the chorus of religion bashing by describing the Hindu faith as "wicked," "pagan," and "evil." For Hindus around the world, the political impact of the statement was equivalent to a category five hurricane.

Sorry Dave, you have been drinking. The religion is called Hinduism, not Hindu. But that's okay. When the mind is befuddled, it is hard to remember people, especially a man by the name of Gandhi, one of the greatest exponents of peace in modern times. Yet thousands of years before you uttered those very words, Hinduism had always claimed the existence of only one God.

When you wake up to the realization of a world outside the United States, please come by and have a look at the Great Banyan, the mother of all banyan trees and a living spectacle for tourists at the botanical gardens on the outskirts of Calcutta, India.

From a distance, the Great Banyan appears to be a forest of trees, but in reality it is a single tree with many individual trunks bigger than the size of an average living room. New shoots grow upward for ordinary trees, but the banyan sends them downward from its branches. These aerial shoots then turn into new trunks as they reach the ground. The Great Banyan has about three thousands of them.

With a canopy that extends more than the size of three soccer fields, the Great Banyan is one of the widest trees in the world. A true survivor, it has withstood the onslaught of the weather and disease for over 200 years. Among the banyans, it is the oldest in the land. It is ironic that the revered banyan produces a lot of red fruit that is utterly useless. No one wants to eat them, although they are prized by the nearby monkeys and some tourists.

The Great Banyan

For the Hindus, the banyan[1] is sacred, but I believe it's more than that. The tree is a true embodiment of the religion. Just as thousands of trunks support the banyan, many age-old traditions and beliefs, often in conflict with one another, sustain the world's oldest living religion.

---

1 Among the sacred trees of India, the pipal comes first and is the king of the trees. This is the same bodhi tree under which Buddha achieved enlightenment. Next is the banyan. Uniquely Indian, the banyan is mentioned in the Hindu mythologies and Jataka tales, where many of the colourful characters used the shade of the tree for meetings, meditation, and rest.

You will be surprised to learn that while most Hindu traditions promote peace, others sacrifice animals to appease gods. When sections of the society are pure vegetarians, some regions are famed for their meat-based cuisines.

Over the years, Hinduism has been attacked, both from inside and outside. It has gone through periods of decay and disarray. Yet like the banyan, it has continued to adapt, survive, and thrive. Centuries-old customs like Sati or bride burning have been outlawed. The caste system, a permanent blot on the religion, is in decline. Older gods like Indra and Mitra were driven to obscurity, and gods like Vishnu and Ganesha have gained prominence. Despite the multiplicity of gods, Hinduism has always stated that Krishna and Shiva and Lakshmi and Saraswati are merely different names for the one and only absolute reality called Brahman.

For an outsider trying to understand Hinduism, the religion is utterly confusing. Some describe Hinduism as an all-absorbent sponge, while others liken it to an impenetrable jungle. Most outsiders, like Dave, are too wrapped up in their own religion and can only see as far as the forest, and then make sweeping generalizations.

> *As long as the Hindu race does not forget the great inheritance of their forefathers, no power on earth could destroy them*
> – Vivekananda (1863–1902)

4

Fast Facts on Hinduism

Founder: None

Size Rank: Third-largest religion in the world with about one billion adherents. Eighty percent of the world Hindu population lives in India. There are significant Hindu populations in the United Kingdom and the United States.

Date of Origin: No specific date. Studies on ancient speech patterns indicate an origin of about 1500 BCE, while archeological evidence points to a much older origin, around 4000 BCE.

Holy Book: No single sacred book considered the most holy, like the Bible. Popular sacred books include the Vedas, Bhagavad Gita, and the epics Mahabharata and Ramayana

Religious Leader: No one religious figure considered the leader of Hinduism. Hinduism had several prominent sages and philosophers throughout its history, and recent ones include Ramakrishna, Vivekananda and Gandhi

Holy Place: No one religious site is considered the most holy. Among the thousands of holy places, seven ancient cities of India are considered the holiest, with Kashi (Varanasi, India) the greatest among them.

Doctrine: No single doctrine. Core concepts of Hinduism include karma, religious duty (dharma), liberation of soul (moksha), and reincarnation (samsara).

Religious Symbol: No one religious symbol. The Om and the Swastika are widely recognized symbols of Hinduism

Place of Origin: Ancient India—the area now occupied by India, Pakistan, Afghanistan, and Bangladesh.

Number of Gods: 330 million (personal gods) by some estimates.

Major Sects: Saivism, Vaishnavism, Saktism, and Smarta

Popular Festivals: Hinduism is often described as a religion of fasts, feasts, and festivals. Key festivals are Diwali (festival of lights), Holi (festival of colors), Shivaratri, and Dassera

5

The United States of India

> *India is an abstraction ... India is no more a political personality than Europe. India is a geographical term. It is no more a united nation than the Equator.*
>
> – Winston Churchill (in 1931)

Let's take a trip back into history. It's the late 1940s and the British Raj has ended. The 600-odd princely states in the region of India are faced with a difficult choice. Should they join the greens or the saffrons? Can they remain independent or form a union of their own?

In a defining moment in history, 565 princely states along with the colonial provinces united to form the independent nation of India in a land roughly one-third the size of the United States. From the sidelines emerged a nation called Pakistan, a new Muslim country carved out of the Indian region because of religious schism at that time.

In the days after independence, India was sliced and diced, and cleaved and coalesced. The political boundaries were redrawn, and they continue to change even now. Modern India is a union of seven union territories and twenty-eight states, the last two states joining the federation only in 2000. It is home to more than a billion people of various ethnic, linguistic, and religious backgrounds.

India opted for a parliamentary system of democracy based on the British Westminister system. Its federal system of government is similar to that of the United States, but unlike America, the central government has greater power in relation to the states. In the period since independence, the central government has dismissed state governments unable to muster a majority or under specific constitutional clauses and placed them directly under the president's rule.

Soon after achieving independence, India became a republic with a president as the formal head of state. Without a king or queen at the helm, Indians dispensed with the need for butlers and their steamy bestsellers. Many distinguished Indians—Hindu, Muslim, Sikh, and most recently a woman—have served the office of the president. Elected for a term of five years, the president is only a figurehead. Usually clad in a Sherwani suit, the president presents himself on formal occasions and carefully utters modulated banalities from a prepared manuscript. The real decision maker is the prime minister and the cabinet of ministers.

Although Hindus form 82 percent of the population, India is secular by constitution, meaning equality of all religions. At the center of the Indian flag is depicted the spoked wheel of Ashoka Chakra, a Buddhist symbol dating back to 200 BCE, symbolizing India's strong ties with the Buddhist faith. The nation's motto states, "Satyameva Jayate," meaning truth alone triumphs. India is also a socialist country providing social and economic equality for its citizens, but that exists only in theory. Fraud by middlemen is rampant in the welfare system. As a result, India has become the slum capital of the world and the land of slumdog millionaires. The judiciary resembles the western system; however, judges, not juries, conduct trials.

As for the relationship between India and Pakistan, the less said the better. United by history but divided by destiny, the two sibling nations have been locked in fierce rivalry since their formation. They have fought three wars, two of which were over the disputed region of Kashmir. Nowadays when Pakistan sneezes from a cold, gets a hangnail, or stubs its toe, the blame goes to India. If India splits its hair or trips over its shoelaces, it is believed to be the work of Pakistani undercover agents. The seeds of rivalry hark back to the days of partition.

At the time of partition, not all rulers of the princely states were particularly keen about merging their domains with India and hoisting the saffron flag. Two states presented unique problems.

One was Hyderabad, which was located in the center of India and ruled by a Muslim sovereign over a predominantly Hindu population. The other was the picturesque Kashmir, where a Hindu sovereign controlled a Muslim majority. While Hyderabad was forcibly annexed to the Indian union at that time, Kashmir is still the subject of a protracted dispute, and the issue is still pending at the UN Security Council. Parts of Kashmir are today controlled by three countries: India (Jammu and Kashmir), Pakistan (north and western regions), and China (north-eastern region called Aksai Chin).

Today India is one of the fastest-growing economies in the world, and Pakistan is an emerging economy. Both are members of the nuclear club. Both have undergone periods of political instability. While Pakistan succumbed to fanaticism and inherited a legacy of dictatorship, India preserved its democratic system with changes occurring in a more or less orderly manner. India has an advanced space program and has sent an unmanned probe to the moon. Pakistan, on the other hand, has a dismembered civil society. While India made rapid strides in information technology, two Pakistani brothers unleashed the world's first computer virus.

It may appear India was the major beneficiary at the partition, for India got the major cities, the main industrial hub, and 95 percent of hydroelectric power stations. Pakistan inherited a large semi-desert with eighty million people. The only important city was Lahore. The Hindus who migrated to India were professionals and artisans, but the ones who settled into Pakistan were mostly laborers.

While the former frontiers of India went beyond Afghanistan, today it is only a shadow of its old self. The river Indus from the "Land of Seven Rivers" now flows mostly through Pakistan. As archaeological excavations and satellite imaging carried out in the 1980s would reveal, what India lost at the partition was the very cradle of the Hindu world and the historical center of civilization. Stay tuned.

What is colonial India?

Colonial India popularly refers to the period between 1510 and 1961 CE.

Portuguese India	1510 – 1961
Dutch India	1605 – 1825
Danish India	1696 – 1869
French India	1759 – 1954
East India Company	1612 – 1757
Company Rule in India	1757 – 1857
British Raj	1858 – 1947 (Queen Victoria proclaimed Empress of India)
Independent India	1947 – present

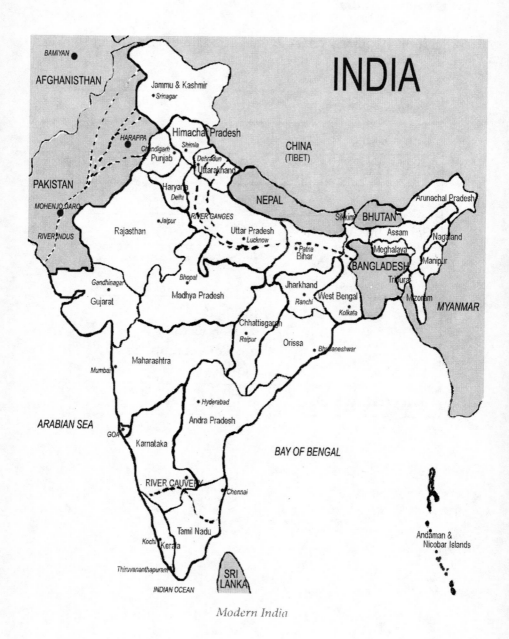

Modern India

6

Who is a Hindu?

S omewhere I read that Hindus are born into the religion, and I had
agreed. The incredibly long names of Sivaya Subramuniyaswami
and Vamadeva Shastri conjured up images of Hindu holy men with
hoary beards chanting hymns at a holy temple somewhere in India.

I was wrong. Traditionally, one must be born into the religion to be a
Hindu. A Hindu is someone whose parents are also Hindus. Tradition
says every Tom, Dick, or Cathy, however learned or devoted but born
outside the religion, must wait until another lifetime to enter the faith,
right? That was tradition; however, the time of tradition is clearly behind
us, for nothing in the scripture says a Hindu must be born into the religion.

Historically, Hinduism hasn't been a proselytizing religion. Of all the
rocks on which the religion is built, the harmony of religious beliefs is
a central part of Hinduism. "Truth is one, but sages call it by different
names," says the Vedas. Not only did Hinduism accept the legitimacy of
other religions, it also offered its devotees the freedom to follow any path
to god. With the coming of Buddhism and Jainism around 600 BCE,
many Hindus converted to these newly found religions.

The need for a break in tradition and formal entrance into the religion
did not arise until late into the 19th century. Until then, the outside world
hardly knew anything about the religion. Even though Hinduism was
sympathetic to those leaving the religion, it literally bolted its doors to
outsiders for centuries. Entry into the religion was further complicated

by the question of caste. With the conquest of India around 1000 CE by Muslim rulers, Islam set its foot in the country. And during the colonization of India in the 16th century, Christianity began to flourish in the subcontinent. All these times, the tradition of being born into the religion continued with Hinduism.

Unlike Hinduism, Christianity and Islam were proselytizing religions and made systematic efforts at gaining converts. With the arrival of Christian missionaries in India, conversion began with a fervor never seen in the history of the nation. Indoctrinated by the missionaries that the only hope of achieving salvation and thereby securing a place in heaven is by proselytizing, every new convert pressed in earnest to bring his immediate family and friends into the Christian fold.

Soon Hindus began to lament on the impact of Christian missionaries amid cries of "spiritual colonialism" and "cultural invasion." The increasing contact of Hindu thinkers with Western thought during this period led to the emergence of a number of reform movements. Although orthodox Hindus remain opposed to the idea, Hindu scholars and philosophers slowly began to warm up to the idea of accepting outsiders into the religion.

An informal method of induction into the religion began with the Arya Samaj, a Hindu reform of the 19th century. Called "Shuddhi Karma" or purification ceremony, the program was aimed at bringing back Hindus who had converted to Islam and Christianity.

By the late 19th century, a global phenomenon was taking place. Hinduism began to receive worldwide attention through Swami Vivekananda, the first Hindu missionary to the West and the man credited with bringing world status to the religion. Throngs of Western devotees were attracted to Hinduism and flocked to Ramakrishna Order, a reform movement founded by Swami Vivekananda. Many of them, although not born into the religion, accepted Hindu names and went on to take formal lifelong vows of celibacy and asceticism.

Today you can become a Hindu by adopting a Hindu name. Most people, however, prefer formal entrance and initiation and a number of Hindu organizations, such as the Arya Samaj or Himalayan Academy, assist with the entry of non-Hindus into the religion. The process essentially consists of the legal adoption of a Hindu name and the undertaking of the traditional Hindu name-giving ceremony of

"Namakaran." A certificate attesting the sworn religion can be handy particularly prior to exchanging Hindu wedding vows or for entry into a few South Indian temples. Once you have officially joined the Hindu fold, it's time to honor the age-old Hindu tradition by mounting an idol of Lord Ganesha in your car. From now on, may all your journey be auspicious ☺.

Another form of entry into the religion that has gained popularity within the past decade is through ethical conversion in which all ties with past faiths are severed. Krishna Prem, Sivaya Subramuniyaswami, Vamadeva Shastri and many others, including George Harrison of the Beatles, belong to this new breed of Westerners who have embraced Hinduism wholeheartedly by abandoning their ties with their Western traditions.

Times have changed. Although mainstream Hinduism does not proselytize, some sects of the religion, like the Hare Krishna group, actively engage in proselytizing. Today you can be a born, a made, or an ethical Hindu. The doors of Hinduism are open to just about everyone, regardless of their past faiths or beliefs, prompting Robin Zaehner, a British academic, to say, "If anyone feels excluded from the Hindu embrace, it is by his or her own choice."

7

Icons of India

> *We owe a lot to the Indians, who taught us how to count, without which no worthwhile scientific discovery could have been made.*
> – Albert Einstein (1879–1955)

India evokes a distinct set of emotions and imagery in people. While many are fascinated by the land of Bengal tigers, the rich heritage of Indian dances, and the Eastern mysticism, some fear India as the outsourcing giant that destroys jobs in their countries and deprives them of their right to live a dignified life.

Here are ten things associated with India:

1. Taj Mahal. Every Westerner either has visited already or wants to visit Taj in the future. Voted recently as one of the new Seven Wonders of the World, the Taj Mahal was built by Shah Jahan, a 17th century Muslim king in Hindu-dominated India, in memory of his wife Mumtaz Mahal, who died while delivering their 14th child.

2. Yoga. Synonymous with India, this ancient Hindu philosophy was formalized by sage Patanjali as a means to seek union with God. In modern times, the physical aspect of yoga has gained prominence and has become an important component in fitness regimes and breathing exercises.

3. Mahatma Gandhi. The English-educated barrister was often said to be born in India, but made in South Africa. Known as the father of the nation of India, Mahatma Gandhi won independence from the British in 1947 through nonviolence. He was the pioneer of Satyagraha, the resistance to authority by mass civil disobedience.

4. Namaste. The Indian way of greeting each other whether you are in the streets, at a house, or on the phone. Namaste has a deep spiritual significance and is a "meeting of the minds," and it is accomplished by placing the folded palms placed before the chest.

5. Himalayas. The highest mountain range in the world is also home to Mount Everest (in neighboring Nepal), the highest mountain peak of the world, and one of the popular destinations of tourists and adventure seekers. Such is the might of the Himalayan range that there are more than one hundred separate mountains in the Himalayas with peaks exceeding 7,200 meters. (The largest peak outside the Himalayan range is 6,962 meters.)

6. Kama Sutra. Written by sage Vatsyayana between the 1st and 6th centuries, the Kama Sutra is an ancient Indian text on sex, widely considered the standard work on love in the Sanskrit literature. The reliefs on the famous temples of Khajuraho, Madhya Pradesh, bear testimony to the enshrining spirit of love and have been called the Kama Sutra in stone.

7. Sari. Although Indian clothing is popular for its dazzling colors, none can beat the six-yard sari, the dress worn by millions of women. Sari lends both grace and glamour and epitomizes the continuity of an age-old India tradition that has withstood the onslaught of many different cultures.

8. Bindi. A red vermilion dot, worn on the forehead between the eyebrows, is considered a major nerve point in the human body by the Hindus. Traditionally a symbol of marriage, the bindi has now become a decorative item and is worn by most Indian women, married and unmarried, Hindus and others.

9. Curry. With origins in India, curry was brought to the West by the British colonists in India during the 18th century. Nowadays curry has

been adopted into all of the mainstream cuisines of the Asian region, and, along with tea, is one of the few food items truly Asian.

10. Ayurveda. A philosophy that deals with the quality of life, Ayurveda is the oldest known form of health care in the world and traces its roots to the Vedic period (1500 BCE) in ancient India. Ayurveda is applied not only to treat diseases but also to maintain health, and is based on the concept that all diseases begin with an imbalance or stress in the individual's consciousness.

Now to some of the lesser known icons associated with India …☺

11. Loos. While India boasts many world-famous tourist destinations, entry to these attractions is often lined up with the world's filthiest toilets. India (along with neighboring China) leads the charge of having the world's grottiest toilets.

12. Paan. The betel-leaf snack, often used as a mouth freshener, is the favorite after-meal snack of Indians. Evidence of its popularity can be seen in the corridors of government buildings, toilets, streets, and most public places.

> *There are some parts of the world that, once visited, get into your heart and won't go. For me, India is such a place. When I first visited, I was stunned by the richness of the land, by its lush beauty and exotic architecture, by its ability to overload the senses with the pure, concentrated intensity of its colors, smells, tastes, and sounds. It was as if all my life I had been seeing the world in black and white and, when brought face-to-face with India, experienced everything re-rendered in brilliant technicolor.*
> – Keith Bellows, National Geographic Society

8

The Elusive Religion

> *Oh, East is East, and West is West, and never the twain shall meet.*
>
> – Rudyard Kipling (1865–1936)

At the top of a roller coaster ride in Disneyland, California, a petrified Indian closes his eyes and invokes the names of Hindu gods, "Yamakandeshwara, Muruga, Paremeshwara. Please be on my side." Not too far away, you can hear his or her Western counterpart screech, "Bloody hell, this is $#%@% awesome!"

At first blush, every person in the West will find Eastern wisdom confusing if not intimidating. Like the left and right sides of the brain, the Eastern and Western hemispheres of the planet appear to be completely different in their thinking. Hindus think their religion is eternal, but others think it is elusive.

Why elusive? First, there's a language barrier to overcome in understanding Hinduism. Ancient Hindu scriptures like the Vedas and the Bhagavad Gita are written in Sanskrit. An officially dead and extinct language, Sanskrit, however, comes naturally to Indians since it is the mother of major North Indian languages like Hindi, Bengali, and Marathi.

Second, the style of presentation of Indian texts is markedly different from their Western counterparts. Seldom would you find a direct, straight-line approach as in Western philosophical texts. Excepting the works of renowned writers, the average written material is circular. They seem to start in the middle instead of defining things from the beginning. And they appear to be convoluted and repetitive to those unfamiliar with the style. You see, Indian thinkers have structured their text to the liking of a Bollywood musical. The main points are sung in chorus, and the supporting ideas and examples are sung repeatedly as stanzas.

Third, the western thought is dominated by reasoning and critical analysis. The Eastern thought, on the other hand, relaxes these criteria and makes liberal use of the mental faculties, such as the mind. For Hindus, the mind is the sixth sense. Concepts like samadhi, consciousness, or nirvana, which refer to different states of the mind, are generously sprinkled into the literature. Indian philosophers rigorously apply these mental faculties in innovative ways to take us into another dimension of our being. If you think reading the Bhagavad Gita is one-dimensional, think again.

Fourth, if text is fraught with difficulties, speech is another kettle of fish. Unlike the speakers or orators of the West, most Indians don't articulate in monotonous tones with subtle variations. Instead conversations are marked with animations, with emotions running free using gestures and mudras. At times during conversation, Indians will pause in midstream to think profoundly of a problem, leaving discussions suspended in mid-air. Then they segue to a different topic without any hesitation.

As if text and speech are not confusing enough, next cultural differences come into play. The one gesture that brings an outsider immediately to his knees is the famous Indian head bobble. Nobody knows what it signifies, for it can mean many things depending on the context. It is the Indian way of answering questions with a yes-roll instead of the usual nod.

Seth Stevenson writes in the online magazine *Slate* about the unique Indian headshake. "I love the Indian head waggle. It's a fantastic bit of body language, and I'm trying to add it to my repertoire. The head waggle says, in a uniquely unenthusiastic way, 'OK, that's fine.' In terms of western gestures, its meaning is somewhere between the nod (though less affirmative) and the shrug (though not quite as neutral). To perform the head waggle, keep your shoulders perfectly still, hold your face completely expressionless, and tilt your head side-to-side, metronome style. Make it smooth—like you're a bobble-head doll. It's not easy. Believe me, I've been practicing."

There are more differences between the East and the West, but the fact is India is different. Like the country, the people are different. Every Westerner who flashes a smile and attempts to spark up a conversation by saying, "How are you this fine morning?" is startled to hear a full list of detailed health complaints from his or her Indian counterpart. Hence it's no surprise that those who have visited India, travelled the vast land, and observed its age-old traditions give up at some point and exclaim, "This place is crazy. It's total chaos!" And they are not wrong.

The truth is both you and I are shaped and influenced by our own culture, which we do not realize until we are confronted with another culture and another way of doing things. It is only when you labor patiently to learn enough of another culture that you will discover the wisdom of their ancestors. From chaos emerges an order. From a cacophony of voices springs a new viewpoint.

Do I sound crazy? Do I look stupid to you? Believe me, every Indian you meet is crazy or stupid from another cultural perspective. Get in step with cultural lunacy, and soon you'll unravel the mystery of the religion.

9

Buddha – The Enlightened One

Bodhisattva, in Buddhism, is an enlightened person who, out of compassion, forgoes nirvana in order to save fellow human beings from the endless cycles of birth and rebirth. Having practiced the virtues of Buddhism over many lifetimes, a bodhisattva has come to this world for the final transmigration of his soul. The most famous among bodhisattvas was undoubtedly Siddharta Gautama, who later came to be known as Buddha or "the enlightened one."

Siddharta was born to a rich ruling family around 563 BCE in what is now modern Nepal. According to legend, he led a sheltered and pampered life in his early years and at sixteen became wedded to a beautiful princess. Not satisfied with the worldly life he enjoyed as a prince, Siddharta occasionally took secret trips outside the palace with his mentor and charioteer to see what was going on in the outside world. During these trips, he witnessed the famous Four Signs, which involved four crucial worldly experiences that affected him profoundly. One involved old age, from which his mentor reminded him there was no escape; another involved disease, which his mentor pointed out may strike anyone regardless of age; the third involved death, which is inevitable for all living beings. The young Siddharta was deeply upset by the suffering he had witnessed. No one could give him an answer as to what could be done about it.

The turning point was the fourth trip in which Siddharta came upon a wandering ascetic, who seemed to radiate peace and serenity despite his difficult existence. He appeared to be detached from the problems and sufferings of life. This encounter gave Siddharta hope that there is a solution to the seemingly inescapable suffering of life. Shortly after his wife had borne him a son, Siddharta abandoned all his worldly existence, including his wife and child, to seek wisdom from the holy men and philosophers of his day. Siddharta had now forever disappeared, for he became the monk Gautama, or as he is still called, Sakyamuni, meaning the ascetic of the Sakyas.

Initially, Buddha joined a religious community where he learned the system of meditation. The path he took was aimed at preparing himself by extreme asceticism and deep meditation for the moment of enlightenment. For a period of six years, Gautama nearly starved himself to death and exposed himself to extreme heat and cold. During this time, he had attracted five followers who joined him in his search for enlightenment. One day to their surprise, Gautama gave up asceticism by accepting a bowl of food, for Gautama was truly convinced that extreme asceticism was not the answer to enlightenment.

His followers deserted him, but Gautama was committed to the pursuit of enlightenment. True enlightened eventually descended on Gautama after another forty-nine days while he was meditating beneath a fig tree, or "Bodhi" tree, at a place called Gaya. It became known as Bodh Gaya, which is now revered by Buddhists as the "Navel of the Earth" on which the holiest shrine, the Mahabodhi temple, stands.

Although interpretations vary on the nature of Buddha's enlightenment, most Buddhist traditions agree that he attained a perfect understanding of each of his previous existences and the reality of samsara—the wheel of life and the material world.

For the rest of his life, Buddha began a path of teaching that lasted some forty years. He travelled to Deer Park in Benares, known today as Varanasi, where he met with his five former disciples who had earlier abandoned him for renouncing extreme asceticism. He taught them the basic teachings of Buddhism, which included the so-called Eightfold Path involving an amalgam of wisdom, meditation, and morality. This path was based on the Four Noble Truths, which, if followed resolutely, will lead to the release from the eternal cycle of death and rebirth.

As an old man, Buddha suffered repeated bouts of debilitating illness and became progressively frail. Shortly before nirvana, he spoke for the last time, saying "All creations are impermanent, work diligently for your liberation."

His death is believed to have occurred in about 483 BCE. After Sakyamuni's death, his disciples elaborated the teachings of Buddha and paved the way for the development of more than a dozen splinter sects. When he died, Buddha had omitted to name a successor. There were no buddha incarnations waiting in the wings nor bodhisattvas preparing for ultimate enlightenment.

Buddhism has since gone through some twenty-five centuries without a central authority. The first split came as early as the fourth century BCE, when Buddhism broke down into two major forms: Theravada and Mahayana. The scriptures of Mahayana are written in Sanskrit, whereas those of Theravada are written in Pali, an ancient Indian dialect. Theravadas remained loyal to the letter of Buddhist teachings and stressed the importance of attaining nirvana through one's own effort without assistance from bodhisattvas. A Theravada Buddhist who attains enlightenment through personal efforts by following the teachings of another is called an arhat, who then attains nirvana at death. Because of its rigorous application, Theravada is concentrated today mainly in Sri Lanka, Burma, Thailand, and few other places.

Unlike Theravada, Mahayana tried to develop the underlying spirit of Buddha's message. Being liberal and democratic, Mahayana evolved continuously over the years and spread into China, Japan, Korea, Tibet, and elsewhere. In Tibet, Buddhist ideas had become the basis for the traditional system of government, run by the Dalai Lama, until the Chinese occupation in 1959. Mahayanas hope to attain nirvana through bodhisattvas and an enlightened Mahayana becomes a buddha. Since buddha refers to a title, there can be any number of buddhas, but only one Buddha, which always refers to Sakyamuni.

> *Buddham Saranam Gacchami*[2]
> *Dhammam Saranam Gacchami*
> *Sangham Saranam Gacchami*

---

2 The Three Jewels of Buddhism are Buddham, the goal we strive to achieve; Dharmam, the teachings that lead to that goal; and Sangham, the community of monks and nuns.

10

The Scorpion and the Turtle

Originally written in Sanskrit and attributed to Vishnu Sharma, the Fables of Bidpai include a story in which a scorpion meets a turtle at the riverbank. In one version of the story, the scorpion, a poor swimmer, asks the turtle, "Will you carry me on your back across to the other side?"

"Are you stupid?" exclaims the turtle. "I've heard plenty of stories about you, scorpions. You are impulsive, psychopathic, and unpredictable. You'll sting me while I'm swimming and I'll drown."

"My dear turtle," pleads the scorpion, "Can't you use some common sense. If I were to sting you, you would drown and I would go down with you. We both would end up very dead!"

The turtle ponders on the scorpion's words. He's right. He can't afford to sting me, so why not ferry him across on my back.

"All right, hop on," says the turtle. The pair starts off across the river, and sure enough, halfway across the river, the scorpion gives the turtle a mighty sting.

As they both sink to the bottom of the river, the turtle cries out, "Why did you do this. It doesn't make sense!" And the scorpion replies, "Life doesn't make sense!"

There comes a time in every person's life when he or she is confronted with the question: What's the purpose of life? Would you be indifferent like the scorpion and consider life meaningless? Or will you be the turtle brimming with kindness and full of hope?

For some, human life is just a biological and social adventure. To science, life means nothing other than going about the business of creating more life. But life is more than just breathing or procreating. The purpose of life, we all agree, is to seek happiness, but happiness is an elusive thing. It appears mysteriously during moments of joy and disappears during times of distress, which makes us wonder whether happiness is really in God's plan of creation.

Will the pursuit of happiness somehow lead to selfishness? Research shows that it is unhappy people who tend to be most self-focused and socially withdrawn. Happy people, on the other hand, are found to be more sociable and tolerant of life's frustrations than unhappy people.

Then, you might ask, "Is it possible to achieve true happiness?" When a Tibetan monk from Dharamsala proclaimed it is possible to transform our attitude and our outlook on life through inner discipline, a crowd of six thousand at Arizona State University, in the United States, stood up and clapped.

And when the saffron-clad monk called Dalai Lama[3] said, "True happiness can be achieved by training the mind," it literally rocked the world.

> *There are only three events in a man's life: birth, life, and death.*
> *He is not conscious of being born, he dies in pain, and he forgets to*
> *live.*
>
> — Jean de la Bruyere (1645–1696)
>
> *Life is a sexually transmitted disease and the mortality rate is one*
> *hundred percent.*
>
> — R.D. Laing (1927–1989)

---

3 The successive Dalai Lamas form a lineage of reborn magistrates of Tibet that traces back to 1391. The current Dalai Lama is Tenzin Gyatso and is the fourteenth one. Tibetian Buddhists believe the Dalai Lamas are incarnations of Avaloitesvara, the bodhisattva of compassion.

11

Some Little-Known Facts on Hinduism

The word "Hinduism" is of recent vintage and was coined by travelers in the 18th and 19th centuries. From ancient times, Hindus call their religion Sanatana Dharma.

- Indians refer to their country as Bharat. Postage stamps of India indicate the same, in the official language of Hindi.

- Although considered the home of Hindus, India has a sizable Muslim population (13 percent) and is the third-largest Muslim country in the world.

- Hinduism is not one religion, but a collection of ancient religious traditions from the Indian subcontinent.

- It is the world's oldest living religion and perhaps the most mature. Considered the mother of all religions, Hinduism is the only religion that openly acknowledges all paths lead to God.

- Although a notable feature of Hinduism is the presence of many, many gods, the scriptures stated thousands of years ago that these gods are manifestations of the one and only supreme reality called Brahman[4]. Hindus identify the many facets of the supreme reality with personal Gods, like Shiva and Krishna, through worship in temples and shrines at home.

- Contrary to popular belief in the West, India is not a Hindu nation by constitution; rather it is a secular country. The only Hindu country in the world was Nepal, which changed into a secular state in 2006.

- The key principle behind Hinduism is cosmic consciousness. Although the religion may appear to be primitive, idolatrous, and polytheistic, some of the concepts are sophisticated and mind-boggling—which we'll soon discover.

- Most major religions, like Christianity, Islam, and Judaism, are dogmatic in the sense that followers must uphold the core principles of the religion else face excommunication or expulsion from the group. There are no dogmas in Hinduism, and you have the freedom to steadfastly hold on to your beliefs or embrace any path. Whether you are an ardent devotee or a dyed-in-the-wool atheist, Hinduism affords the same treatment to you.

- There are no devils or Satan in Hinduism, but you'll find plenty of demons.

- The concept of sin or the idea of eternal hell does not exist in Hinduism.

- Unlike Christians and Muslims, Hindus dispose of dead bodies by cremation. The body is washed with holy water and either burned with a slow fire on a funeral pyre or placed in an electric crematorium.

---

4 The key idea of one god is a theme repeated ad infinitum in this book.

12

Zoroastrianism

On her blog, Zita Scholari notes a few fascinating similarities between the ancient scriptures of Rig Veda and Avesta.

> _The word Hindu itself is actually a Persian word coined by Cyrus the great in the 6th century BCE to describe people who lived beyond the river Sindhu (now Indus), which was the eastern boundary of the ancient Persian empire. The Persians had a phonetic problem with the letter "S", and could only say it as "H". Hence Sindhu became Hindu...._

> _The Avesta describes historical landmarks called Harahwati, Harayu, and Haptahindu. Likewise the Rig Veda mentions Saraswati, Sarayu, and Saptasindhu. Rig Veda's Soma came from the Avesta's Hoama. There is also a similarity of concepts in the Avesta and the Rig Veda, although reversed. In Avesta, ahura is a god. But asura is a demon in Rig Veda. In Avesta, daiva refers to a demon. Thus Indra is a daiva and a demon. In Rig Veda, of course, Indra is a god...._

> _It appears ancient Persians and Indians shared many such fascinating phonetic affinities. It is believed Persia was the melting pot of civilizations and the original home of Aryans. The Avestan language and Sanskrit may have evolved over the same period...._

There was a touch of Persian pride and patriotism in her words, for Zita is one of the last remaining Zoroastrians in this world. Ancient Persia was home to Zoroastrianism, one of the oldest religions of the world. It was the prominent religion of the Persian Empire until the Arab conquest around 650 CE that changed Persia into Islam.

Zoroastrianism was founded by Zarathustra (Zoroaster in Greek) somewhere between 1500 and 1000 BCE. As a young boy, Zoroaster was trained to be a priest, but at the age of twenty, he left home in search of truth against the wishes of his parents. After ten years, his search for truth culminated in a divine vision where he was led to Ahura Mazda, who taught him the cardinal principles of the good religion. Since that revelation, Zoroaster believed he was ordained to preach the wisdom of God. But in the next ten years Zoroaster achieved little success in preaching, converting only one person, his cousin. Success followed Zoroaster when he converted King Vishtaspa to Zoroastrianism after curing the king's favorite horse from paralysis.

Zoroaster upheld the supremacy of Ahura Mazda in the pantheon of deities in Persia existing that time. In Zoroastrianism, there's only one god, Ahura Mazda, the supreme creator, whose nature is expressed in the cult of fire. The world, according to Zoroastrianism, is a combination of good and evil, and creation cannot exist without the presence of both. At the beginning of the creation of this world, Ahura Mazda created two spirits or Mainyus called Spenta Mainyu and Angra Mainyu. Spenta Mainyu is responsible for the good deeds, for he exists in all of us and helps us to see the light within ourselves. Ahriman, on the other hand, is responsible for evil deeds. Thus Zoroastrianism is monotheistic in Ahura Mazda, but dualistic within the twin spirits.

According to Zoroastrianism, each individual holds the key to his destiny by exercising his own free choice between good and evil. When you choose to lead a good life, you will be rewarded and invited to heaven, else you will be punished and sent to hell. Death is only a temporary triumph of the evil spirit Ahriman. After death the soul is allowed to meditate for three days. Judgment takes place at dawn on the fourth morning. If good outweighs evil, the soul is entitled to go to heaven. Otherwise the soul is led to hell.

Zoroastrianism may have been the first monotheistic religion of the world, for it is interesting to note that many of its core beliefs, such as heaven and hell, god and Ahriman, the coming of a savior, etc., can be found in Western religions like Christianity, Judaism, and Islam. The Zoroastrian holy book, Avesta, includes the original words of Zoroaster, preserved in a series of five hymns called the Gathas. Like the Rig Veda, the Avesta was transmitted orally for many centuries before being written.

Fire is a key element to Zoroastrianism. No ritual or ceremony is complete without the presence of fire. The flame is considered a visible sign of Ahura Mazda. According to tradition, fire was used by Ahura Mazda in the creation of human beings, and fire will be used again at the final renovation of the universe. All sacred fires in temples or homes should be kept constantly burning. Extinguishing fire is considered a grave sin in Zoroastrianism. For this reason, Zoroastrians have been called fire-worshipers although fire in itself is not worshiped but rather regarded as a symbol of Ahura Mazda. Most Zoroastrian temples have a fire that continues to burn with priests chanting hymns of God and feeding fire with sandalwood or cedar.

For the Zoroastrians, the earth is sacred. One of the interesting rituals, which our friend Zita calls eco-friendly, is the way they dispose of their dead so as not to pollute nature with rotten flesh. After death, the body is placed naked on the top of open-topped enclosures called Dokhmas or Towers of Silence for vultures to feed on. After the bones are dried in the sun, they are placed into an ossuary at the center of the Tower.

Like mainstream Hindus, Zoroastrians do not proselytize. Interfaith marriages are discouraged. Converts are not accepted, for one has to be born in the religion. Unlike other religions, the faith upholds equality between genders, enabling many women to become working professionals—starting families later in life. All these factors have contributed to the steady decline of the Zoroastrian population. While once Zoroastrians dominated the entire Persian empire, their numbers have dwindled to less than 200,000. Today Zoroastrians can be found in almost every major city in the West, but the major concentrations are still in India and Iran.

> *Zoroastrianism is the oldest of the revealed world-religions, and it has probably had more influence on mankind, directly and indirectly, than any other single faith.*
>
> – Mary Boyce (1920–2006)

13

Parsis – The Jews of India

It's the 8th century CE. A flotilla of seven ships, crowded with people, lands in the coastal kingdom of Gujarat, India, ruled by the Hindu king Jadi Rana. From the ship emerge hundreds of frightened, forlorn people clad in strange clothing. The women among them cover their faces with scarves, while the men carry weapons. The newly arrived people speak a different language and follow a different religion. Originally from ancient Persia, they have fled their country fearing religious persecution from Muslim Arabs, who have invaded and conquered their homeland. They have come to seek asylum in this country, for the Rajput ruler's reputation for fairness was known far beyond the seas.

True to his reputation, Jadi Rana did not disappoint the newly arrived people. The king was not only a just ruler but also a wise one for he was concerned that these refugees speaking a foreign language and following a different culture would become isolated in a Hindu country. Permission for stay was granted on the conditions that they adopt the local language of Gujarati, that women accept the traditional clothing of sari, and that men cease to bear arms henceforth.

And thus began one of the greatest success stories of migration, for these were the group of Zoroastrians who were the ancestors of J.R.D Tata, the father of Indian civil aviation, of Zubin Mehta, the world-renowned conductor, and of Farrokh Bulsara, more popularly known as Freddie Mercury of the rock band Queen, who rocked the world with the song "Bohemian Rhapsody."

The next few centuries saw the assimilation of the Zoroastrians within the Indian society, where they came to be known as Parsis (Persians). Although integrated with predominantly Hindu society, they did not surrender their ethnic identity and tenaciously clung to their religion. The Parsis erected several fire temples, where a flame was always kept burning as a symbol of the life cycle. They also erected the Towers of Silence to leave their dead ones to be devoured by vultures. Suffering no further persecution in India, the Parsis made modest livings out of farming and small trade for centuries. A variation of Gujarati became their mother tongue.

The fortunes of Parsis changed dramatically with the coming of the British. Many Parsis, who until then had been living in farming communities throughout Gujarat, moved to the British-run settlements to take up new jobs. When the British East India Company transferred their headquarters from Surat, Gujarat, to Bombay to set up their first port, the Parsis followed them. Soon they began to occupy positions of trust in the government and public works. The British education system provided the Parsis with an opportunity to learn about the British establishment. The Parsis, in turn, found themselves closer to the British than to any other group and became unswervingly loyal to their masters. For their loyalty, the British rewarded them by granting trade and sole selling agencies.

In business, the Parsis were second to none. Soon they dominated the commercial life of Victorian Bombay, manifesting a business acumen that got them dubbed the "Jews of India." Even today, several of the best-known business conglomerates of India, such as Tata, Godrej, and Wadia, are run by the Zoroastrian-Parsi families. James Mackintosh, the nineteenth-century recorder of Bombay, notes that "the Parsees are a small remnant of one of the mightiest nations of the ancient world … and were for many ages lost in obscurity and poverty, till at length they met a just government under which they speedily rose to be one of the most popular mercantile bodies in Asia."

Today Parsis are the most affluent of the societies of India, one in which you'll find no beggars—until recently. Despite their wealth, Parsis are renowned for their honesty and philanthropy. It is said, "Parsi thy name is Charity." In recent times, however, Parsis have been steadily losing their prosperity and prestige, including their sense of purpose. Nowadays, an increasing number of Parsis in Bombay are on the verge of poverty. Among the young, there is a growing problem of drug addiction. Parsis also are found to have particularly high incidences of mental illness and hemophilia, both perhaps as a result of the close-knit nature of their community as well as inbreeding.

In India their religion is struggling to survive. Moreover, Parsi numbers, which have always been small, are now diminishing at an alarming rate. In 1941 there were about 115,000 Parsis, but by 2001, the figure had fallen to seventy thousand. Non-marriage, marriage into other faiths, and late marriage have all contributed to the decline. Parsi women are highly educated and career-minded, and they tend to postpone family life. In addition, most Parsis in India are migrating to the West. According to internally acclaimed screenwriter Sooni Taraporevala, Parsis will number only twenty-three thousand by the year 2020. With the current trend, Parsis will cease to be called a community and be labeled a "tribe," but they should truly thank the generosity and good heart of Jadi Rana for their survival into the twenty-first century.

> *Whether I am a Hindu, a Mohamedan, a Parsi, a Christian, or of any other creed, I am above all an Indian. Our country is India; our nationality is Indian.*
>
> – Dadabhai Naoroji (1825–1917)

14

Origins of Indian Languages

Separated by some eight thousand kilometers of land and seas, Spain and the Indian state of Bengal are significantly different in their landscape and culture. But when Spaniards and Bengalis start counting, you can't help noticing the striking similarity in sounds.

Bengali: ek, dui, tin, car, panc, choy, sat, at, noy, dosh.
Spanish: uno, dos, tres, cuatro, cinco, seis, siete, ocho, nueve, diez

It's not just between Spain and Bengal. In fact, you'll observe the similarity among all languages in the Indo-European family of languages, including English, Dutch, Spanish, and Indian languages like Hindi, Bengali, and Marathi. What's happening?

Back in the 18th century, the similarity of sounds caught the attention of an English philologist called William Jones, who after studying the similarities in the grammar, syntax, and vocabulary of Sanskrit with classical Greek and Latin, postulated that all three languages shared a common root. According to Jones, they may have descended from a common source. Now Jones was not just an astute observer. In addition to Sanskrit, he had mastered Persian and Arabic languages. Soon his findings led to the discovery of the Indo-European family of languages, the world's largest family embracing the languages of Europe, America, and Asia.

Who were the original Indo-Europeans? When and where did they live? No one knows, for they did not leave any paper trail or artifacts leading to their homeland. So several theories came into existence, some based on linguistic reconstructions, others on mere speculation. Over time, most scholars settled on a theory that placed the original Indo-European homeland somewhere in the Eurasian steppe lands around 3000 BCE. According to this theory, the civilization broke up around 2500 BCE perhaps due to climatic or environmental changes. People left their homeland and migrated in different directions. Some moved into Greece, others went to Italy, while another branch crossed Iran and Afghanistan and eventually reached India.

It is believed that these Indo-Europeans (aka proto Indo-Europeans) brought the Indo-Aryan (Indic) group of languages to India and thereabouts around 1500 BCE. Today an estimated 700 million people speak the North Indian languages of Hindi, Bengali, and Marathi. Along with Urdu and Punjabi, these languages form the major part of the Indic group, the largest subgroup under the Indo-European family (see table). It is believed a particular group, calling itself Arya or "noble," brought with them the earliest portion of a collection of hymns, known as the Rig Veda.

The Rig Veda was composed in a very early form of Sanskrit called Vedic Sanskrit. The Vedas were always taught and remembered orally as a tradition, even though they could be written down after 800 BCE. Although the spoken word helped spread the religion, Vedic Sanskrit started drifting over the years. The Vedas were eventually written down, but soon it became obvious that the divergence was significant. There was an immediate need to stem this drift, for Vedas had to be remembered with absolute accuracy for them to be ritually effective. Along came the grammar of Panini, and Vedic Sanskrit was soon fixed, but in the meantime it acquired a new name and became Classical Sanskrit. Classical Sanskrit survives today, for it remained the language of religion and literature in India for centuries.

Meanwhile, the spoken language had not only changed but split into dialects that eventually grew into separate languages, called Prakrits. It is out of these languages that the modern languages of North India evolved. The first literary documents began to appear around 1200 CE.

The Prakrits also gave rise to Pali and Ardhamagadhi, the languages of Buddhism and Jainism, respectively.

Those who have been to South India will notice that the people of that region speak an entirely different language. Unlike the languages of North India, the South Indian languages have a different grammatical structure and belong to the Dravidian group, with about 225 million speakers in the world. Although the Dravidian languages are found principally in South India, you can find one in Sri Lanka and one in Pakistan. There are about thirty of these languages in all, but just four of them—Tamil, Kannada, Malayalam, and Telugu—account for 95 percent of the speakers.

Evidence suggests the Dravidian languages existed even before the arrival of the Indo-Europeans. They possessed an ancient but unique history of their own, dating back over five thousand years. The Dravidian history, however, credits the invention of the oldest Dravidian tongue (Tamil) to Rishi Agastya, who was one of the most prominent sages of the Vedic period. Apart from language, both North and South India share a common religion and culture. According to this theory, it is likely that at one time, the Dravidian languages were spoken over much of central and perhaps even North India. The Dravidians were then driven south by the Indo-Europeans, with only those living in isolated regions remaining behind. The few pockets of Dravidian-speakers in central India seem to support this theory.

This is the story of the origin of the Indian languages, as taught in academia even today. Did the Indo-Europeans truly migrate from the Steppes to Greece, Rome, and India? Or was this mere speculation, stretching facts to conform with the Eurocentric view of the original homeland. Going by this theory, India was invaded and conquered around 1500 BCE by light-skinned nomads from Europe who entered the region through Persia (Iran). But archeological discoveries that came out in the 20th century shed a completely different light (we'll discuss them in the coming chapters). Moreover, nothing in the Vedic literature mentions a large-scale migration to the East. Nor does the Dravidian literature suggest Dravidians being driven south. Were the Western scholars-cum-missionaries correct but got the dates out of whack, or did they get everything wrong, including the timing?

Unsubstantiated claims and gaping holes in this theory led some scholars to suggest that the original homeland was rooted in perhaps western Asia or the Indian subcontinent.[5] But the powerful images of nomadic Aryans invading the indigenous people is so ingrained among these Eurocentric scholars that they'll do just about anything to justify their continued belief in it.

Inebriated in the exuberance of its own supremacy, the West clings to the flawed Eurocentric version of the theory because unlike you and me, most people are not prepared to accept the truth, even against overwhelming evidence.

> *The Sanskrit language whatever be its antiquity, is of a wonderful structure; more perfect than the Greek, more copious than the Latin, and more exquisitely refined than either, yet bearing to both of them a stronger affinity, both in the roots of verbs and in the forms of grammar, than could possibly have been produced by accident; so strong, indeed, that no philosopher could examine them all three, without believing them to have sprung from some common source, which, perhaps, no longer exists.*
> — Sir William Jones (1746–1794)
>
> *Greek was nothing more than Sanskrit turned topsy-turvy.*
> — James Prinsep (1799–1840)

Table 1 Some Popular Languages and their Families

Family	Subgroup	Branch	Languages
Indo-European	Germanic	Western	English, German, Yiddish, Dutch, Flemish, Afrikaans
Indo-European	Germanic	Northern (Scandinavian)	Swedish, Danish, Norwegian, Icelandic

---

5 India as the cradle of civilization overcomes some major shortcomings of other theories, but a few hiccups prevail in this theory as well, such as the missing horses. Horses and chariots held a prominent place in the Vedic literature. They have yet to be found in sufficient numbers in the excavated sites so far.

Indo-European	Italic		Latin
Indo-European	Romance		Italian, French, Spanish, Portuguese, Romanian
Indo-European	Celtic	Brythonic	Welsh, Breton
Indo-European	Celtic	Goidelic	Irish (Gaelic)
Indo-European	Indo-Iranian	Iranian	Persian, Pashto, Kurdish…
Indo-European	Indo-Iranian	Indic (Indo-Aryan)	Sanskrit, Hindi, Urdu, Bengali, Punjabi, Marathi, Gujarati, Oriya, Bhojpuri, Maithili, Magahi, Rajasthani, Assamese, Kashmiri, Nepali, Sindhi, Sinhalese
Dravidian			Telugu, Tamil, Kannada (Kanarese), Malayalam, Gondi, Tulu
Sino-Tibetan	Sinitic		Chinese
Independent			Japanese

15

Facts About Indian Languages

S anskrit is to India as Latin and Greek are to Europe. It is the mother of North Indian languages like Hindi, Bengali, Marathi, Punjabi, and Gujarati. Languages like Nepali (Nepal), Urdu (Pakistan), and Sinhalese (Sri Lanka) were also born out of Sanskrit.

Sanskrit belongs to the Indo-European family of languages, which include English, German, Spanish, etc., and was brought to India from the northwest between 2500-1500 BCE, according to our Eurocentric theory of the origin of Indian languages. Classified as one of the twenty-three official languages of India, Sanskrit is a classical and liturgical language of Hinduism, Buddhism, Sikhism, and Jainism. As a spoken language, Sanskrit lost ground to its descendants, but there have been a number of attempts at revival by the government of India. Remarkably, several thousand people still claim Sanskrit as their mother tongue.

About 75 percent of India speaks languages that are descendants of Sanskrit, while the rest speaks any of the four major Dravidian languages. Among Sanskrit's descendants, Bengali, Assamese, Konkani and Marathi still retain a large Sanskrit vocabulary base, while Hindi and Urdu have become diluted with Arabic and Persian influence. Among the Dravidian languages, Malayalam, Telugu, and Kannada also combine a great deal of Sanskrit vocabulary.

Sanskrit is written in an alphabet known as Devanagiri. The English words Brahmin, mantra, and karma are of Sanskrit origin.

Hindi The most widely spoken language of India, even though less than half the population speak the language. The word "Hindi" comes from the Sanskrit word "Sindhu." The Zoroastrians, who were ancient India's immediate neighbors, referred to the people that lived near the Sindhu River as "Hindu," since "Sindhu" is pronounced as "Hindu" in Avestan (the language of ancient Zoroastrians). The land where the Hindus lived became Hindustan.

Nowadays, speakers of Hindi can be found in such far-flung places as Mauritius, Fiji, South Africa, Kenya, Trinidad, Guyana, and Suriname. Hindi is an official language of India and is almost identical to Urdu, the official language of Pakistan. Urdu contains more words from Persian and Arabic and is written in Perso-Arabic script, whereas Hindi is written in Devanagari alphabet. It is interesting to note that Hindi and Urdu were together referred to as Hindustani prior to the partition of India in 1947.

Although the government of India imposed the adoption of Hindi as an official language at the central government, it was met with widespread resistance from non-Hindi speaking states, particularly Tamil Nadu. Today Hindi, along with English, shares the title of official language at the central government.[6] In 1996, prime minister Deva Gowda, who knew little Hindi, addressed the nation in Hindi at the independence-day anniversary by reading a prepared manuscript written in Kannada.

When North Indians and South Indians meet informally, the language of conversation is not Hindi but English.

There are about 420 million speakers of Hindi, with most concentrated in the states of Uttar Pradesh and Madhya Pradesh. English words of Hindi origin include cot, loot, thug, bandanna, dungaree, rajah, guru, juggernaut, and chutney.

Bengali The language of the Indian state of West Bengal, spoken by about eighty million people. Another 120 million from Bangladesh (originally East Bengal), which split from Pakistan in 1972, also speak Bengali, although Bangladeshis prefer to call their language Bangla.

---

6 India has two official languages (Hindi and English) imposed by the Union government. States legislate their own official languages, so the number of official languages has jumped to twenty-three.

Bengali ranks sixth among all languages of the world; only Chinese, Spanish, English, Hindi, and Arabic have more native speakers.

The national anthem of India, "Jana Gana Mana," is written in a Sanskritized version of Bengali. Similarly, the national song of India "Vande Mataram," composed by Bankim Chandra Chattopadhyay, is also written in Sanskritized Bengali.

The alphabet is based on a variation of Devanagari Sanskrit. Bungalow is an English word with Bengali origin.

Punjabi The official language of the Indian state of Punjab and its shared state capital Chandigarh. It is also spoken in the Pakistan province of Punjab. In India, Punjabi is also spoken in the neighboring states of Haryana and Himachal Pradesh.

There are about one hundred million speakers of Punjabi, of which seventy-five million are from Pakistan and the rest, twenty-five million from India. In Pakistan, it is the language of about half the population. Punjabi is also spoken in countries where Punjabis have emigrated in large numbers, including the United States, Australia, the United Kingdom, and Canada. It is the preferred language of most Sikhs. The famous Indian dance called Bhangra is composed in Punjabi.

Punjabi is closely associated with the Sikh religion. Its alphabet, known as Gurumukhi, was invented by the second of the Sikh gurus in the sixteenth century. In Pakistan, Punjabi is written in the Perso-Arabic script, like Urdu.

Marathi Spoken in the Indian state of Maharashtra, which hosts the city of Mumbai and Pune, the center of Marathi culture. A dialect of Marathi known as Konkani is spoken in southwest Maharashtra. Like Bengali literature, Marathi literature is the oldest among the regional literatures in Indo-Aryan languages, dating back to 1000 CE.

The grammar and syntax derives from Pali or Prakrit, although the alphabet is essentially the same as that used in Hindi. There are about seventy-five million speakers of Marathi.

Gujarati Spoken principally in the state of Gujarat, the birthplace of Mahatma Gandhi and Mohammad Ali Jinnah, the fathers of the Indian and Pakistani nations respectively. Gujarati descended from Sanskrit and is written in an alphabet similar to that of Hindi without the head stroke.

Today, you'll find a large number of Gujaratis living in the United Kingdom and in North America. Most of them migrated there from East Africa, under increasing discrimination and pressured by the policies of Africanization, which left them with an uncertain future and citizenship.

There are about fifty million speakers of Gujarati. The English word tank has a Gujarati origin.

Telugu Spoken primarily in the state of Andhra Pradesh. It is also spoken among a diaspora population in the United States, Malaysia, Mauritius, South Africa, Ireland, Fiji, Trinidad, and the United Kingdom. With about seventy-five million speakers, Telugu appears to be the most widely spoken language among the Dravidian languages.

Telugu is one of the most used languages of Carnatic music, the classical music of South India. It is largely Sanskritized and has a wide variety of words of Sanskrit or Prakrit origin. Telugu is generally considered the Dravidian language with the most Indo-Aryan influence.

The Telugu alphabet developed out of ancient Brahmi script, which is considered the mother of virtually all the alphabets of India.

Kannada Also known as Kanarese, it is spoken in southwestern India, principally in the state of Karnataka. Kannada is also spoken in the neighboring states of Andhra Pradesh, Maharashtra, Tamil Nadu, Kerala, and Goa. There are sizable Kannada-speaking communities in the United States, the United Kingdom, and Singapore. A member of the Dravidian family of languages, it is spoken by about forty million people. Native speakers of Kannada are called Kannadigas.

The Kannada alphabet is very similar to that of Telugu.

Tamil Spoken primarily in the Indian state of Tamil Nadu. There are about sixty-five million speakers of Tamil, sixty million from India, and five million from Sri Lanka. It's also widely spoken in Malaysia and Singapore. Tamil was the first Indian language to be declared a classical language by the government of India.

Tamil is the oldest and the most richly developed of the Dravidian languages and has a literary tradition of over two thousand years. Tamil, along with other Dravidian languages, has been greatly influenced by

Sanskrit in terms of vocabulary, grammar, and literary styles. A number of Sanskrit loan words were also absorbed into Tamil, but some native authors tried to resist this trend, culminating in the puristic movement of the twentieth century. As a result, modern Tamil is devoid of Sanskrit loan words in formal documents, public speeches, and scientific discourses. It is estimated that the number of Sanskrit loan words in Tamil may actually have come down from about 50 to 20 percent.

The alphabet, like all other indigenous alphabets of India, is derived from the ancient Brahmi script. The words curry and mulligatawny come from the Tamil language.

Malayalam Spoken in the southern Indian state of Kerala. The word Malayalam is also a palindrome. A native speaker of Malayalam is called a "Malayali" or, more affectionately, a "Mallu." It is also spoken widely in Mahe, in the islands of Lakshadweep, and by a large population of Indian expatriates living in the Middle East.

Malayalam is a Dravidian language. Closely related to Tamil, Malayalam shares similar origins and has a script of its own, covering all the symbols of Sanskrit as well as special Dravidian letters. About thirty-seven million people speak the language.

English words like teak, copra, and atoll come from Malayalam.

16

Indus Valley Civilization

The Indus, from where India gets its name, originates in the foothills of the Karakoram mountains and flows southwest of India through Pakistan. Passing around the hills of Baluchistan before emptying into the Arabian Sea near the port city of Karachi, the Indus is an important river today for the agricultural economies of the subcontinent. Although most tourists are amazed by the sight and sound of gushing water as it meanders through the landscape, unknown to them is the fact that the river holds the key to a lost civilization that once flourished on its banks.

Back in 1944, Sir Mortimer Wheeler, the newly appointed British director of archeology in India, began excavations of a vast mound on the banks of this river. Beneath many layers of soil, he discovered the foundations of an early Bronze Age city, built of fired bricks and arranged in a meticulous grid pattern. Wheeler established that this city of Mohenjo Daro was at least five thousand years old. At about the same time, his archeological teams unearthed an equally impressive urban center called Harappa, about 350 miles to the northeast. Little did Wheeler realize that these discoveries would lead to the greatest controversy to rock the modern world.

The uncovering of these two ancient cities, now located in modern Pakistan, had actually begun much earlier. In the 1820s an English soldier who had deserted the East India Company's army travelled to

Punjab, where he first encountered the remains of Harappa. Noticing a large number of fine and standard-size bricks, he described the site as a "ruinous brick castle" with high walls and towers. In the late 18th century, Sir Alexander Cunningham, the first director general of the Archaeological Survey of India, made several visits to Harappa himself. During his third trip, he was surprised to notice British engineers utilizing the ancient bricks from these ruins as ballast under the tracks for building the railway line between Lahore and Multan.

The bricks were disappearing fast, and so was the need for urgent excavations. From 1900, several excavations were conducted under a young archeologist called John Marshall. It was during this time that Mohenjo Daro was first discovered, but D.R. Bhandarkar, Marshall's deputy, thought the ruins were only 200 years old. Fortunately, this assessment was later reversed to five thousand years. Marshall, along with his Indian deputies, worked diligently with hundreds of laborers on the Mohenjo Daro site. It is said that when Marshall left India he "left India two thousand years older than he found it."

The discovery of new sites continues even today. A recent count shows that as many as 1,400 Indus sites have been found, of which 917 are in India, 481 in Pakistan, and one in Afghanistan. From the works of Marshall and Wheeler and from recent excavations, we can conclude that the Indus Valley Civilization developed around five thousand years ago on the banks of the Indus river flood plain. These settlements covered a remarkable region, almost 1.5 million square kilometers of land, spreading over Afghanistan, Pakistan, and India. In size, the Indus Valley dwarfed the contemporary civilizations of the Nile Valley in Egypt and the Tigris and Euphrates valleys in Sumer (modern Iraq).

It is believed that the cities of the Indus Valley Civilization were well-organized and solidly built out of stones and standardized bricks. They had large and complex hill citadels, housing palaces, granaries, and public baths. The most outstanding of the baths was the great bath of Mohenjo Daro. Beyond the citadels were well-planned towns, laid out in rectangular patterns. The houses were often two-storied and spacious and lined the town streets. Archeologists say the Indus people couldn't have copied their town planning from Egypt and Mesopotamia because in those civilizations the roads meandered like village streets. The drainage comprised brick-lined sewers and was one of the most sophisticated in the ancient world. Compared with the cities of medieval Europe or modern India, Harappa and Mohenjo Daro were much cleaner.

It seems the economy of the Indus civilization was based on highly organized agriculture. Commerce was active and connected to the ancient civilizations of Mesopotamia. The arts flourished and many objects of copper, bronze, and pottery, including a large collection of terra-cotta toys, have been uncovered. The most notable from the ruins of Mohenjo Daro and Harappa are the nearly two thousand inscribed steatite or soapstone seals. Some symbols of religious art with close Hindu associations can be found on seals. These include the pipal and banyan trees, commonly found in Hindu mythology. Many abstract symbols and geometric designs have also been found, including the endless-knot, the swastika, and the circle. However, extensive religious monuments, like the Egyptian pyramids or the Sumerian ziggurats, have been absent in the Indus Valley.

Despite the uncovering of a treasure of artifacts from the ruins, the entire collection pales in comparison with those of ancient Egypt in terms of overall grandeur and magnificence. This is especially marked in the art of sculpture, where the Harappan heritage has just eight major items. The famous of them includes the solid figure of the robed priest-king and the figurine of the so-called Dancing Girl of Mohenjo Daro. In other sites, terracotta figures depicting the Hindu yoga postures (asanas) and traditional greeting of Namaste were found.

What eventually led to the sudden decline of the Indus Valley cities is still not fully understood. Their downfall as urban centers, which seems to have begun in 1900 BCE, may have been partly due to their topographical positioning, since the Indus Valley is subject to frequent flooding.

The discovery of the Indus Valley Civilization raises new questions about our ancestors and heritage. Did the invading Aryans on fast horse-drawn chariots kill the Harappans? Did the fusion of this ancient culture with that of the invading Europeans result in the Indo-Aryan stock that forged the greatest religion of Hinduism? Were the Indus Valley people indigenous Dravidians who were pushed down into South India? Or could the Bronze Age Harappans be Aryans themselves?

The Harappans possessed a script, which they used for inscribing on a variety of objects numbering more than four thousand. They are usually short, made up of twenty-six characters written mostly in one line. Since the sites were discovered, there has been no dearth of claimants purporting to decipher the script. Over a hundred theories have been put forward and even high-speed computers employed, yet not one of them has successfully deciphered the script. It is believed only a bilingual text, one using the Harappan script against another, already known script, would unravel the mystery, in the same way as the decryption of the Rosetta Stone[7] in Egypt, containing the same text in three languages, solved the puzzle of the hieroglyphs.

These inscriptions hold the key. When the Harappan script is truly decrypted, it will uncover our forgotten past and point us to our true ancestors. Until that day dawns, it's worthwhile listening to the gush of the mighty Indus than to idle speculation in classrooms.

> *Half the work that is done in this world is to make things appear what they are not.*
>
> – Elias Root Beadle (1812–1879)

---

7 No one could decipher the Egyptian hieroglyphics until Napoleon Bonaparte discovered the nearly four-foot-tall Rosetta Stone in 1799. That stone placed the until-then unknown hieroglyphics alongside two known languages.

17

Hindus Around the World

Having seen Indians residing in Britain, in the United States, and in far-flung places like Fiji, Trinidad, and Surinam, I sometimes wonder whether Neil Armstrong, while planting the American flag on the moon, might have run into a few illegal Indians settled there. Among the estimated sixty million living abroad, Hindus can be found in large numbers living in the United States and in the United Kingdom. Indeed, the world is teeming with Indians that the only places you don't find them are in the Arctic and the Antarctic regions. Yet I wouldn't be shocked to find a fellow desi[8] settled in an igloo watching a Bollywood kitsch with his yaar.

Statistically speaking, one out of every six people of the world is an Indian. So it's no coincidence that Hindus, who comprise more than 80 percent of the Indian population, are found all over the globe. How did the original Hindus from the Indian subcontinent migrate to other parts of the world?

Movements of Indian Hindus to other parts of the globe can be traced back to the early centuries of the Common Era. Even though Hindus have been migrating in drops and trickles and torrents, the bulk of Hindu migration occurred in three stages.

The first stage of migration happened about 100 CE, when the Brahmins of India migrated to Southeast Asia, in the present regions

---

8 Desi: (slang) a person of Indian descent

comprising Cambodia, Thailand, and the Hindu enclave of Muslim Indonesia called Bali. The Brahmins were invited by the local rulers to consecrate their kingdoms, where they introduced Hindu deities and scriptures. The significance of Brahma in Dheva Sataran temple in Bangkok and in Thailand's royal ceremonies can be seen even today. The annual performance of Ramayana is an established tradition in both Thailand and Indonesia.

It was also during this phase that Tamil Chettiars, a South Indian banking community from Chettinad, Tamil Nadu, expanded their business to Burma, Malaysia, Mauritius, and other parts of the region. They continued their presence over centuries and played a prominent role particularly in Burma, where they were hailed as the crucial providers of finance that turned Burma into the "rice-bowl" of the British Empire. The Chettiars were property owners in Burma, but after Burma's independence in 1948, they were demonized as rapacious usurers and their properties appropriated by the state.

The second phase of migration originated during the colonial regime (1510–1961) mainly in the form of laborers working on the sugar, tea, and rubber plantations of other British colonies. Contract labor was used for work in Burma, Malaysia, and Sri Lanka, while indentured labor (a new form of labor that replaced slavery) was employed for work in the West Indian colonies, Fiji, Mauritius, and South Africa. In Trinidad, Indians did well in the economic arena and dominated in industry and entrepreneurial enterprises, although a minuscule population of whites continue to control the banks and financial services. Famous West Indian cricketers like Shivnarine Chanderpaul, Alvin Kallicharran, Rohan Kanhai, and Ramnaresh Sarwan are all of Indian descent.

The early part of the 20th century witnessed the migration of Gujaratis and Punjabis to the fast-growing towns of Kenya, Uganda, Tanganyika (Tanzania), and Nyasaland (Malawi). Although the Indians established themselves in business and trade, they were soon seen as marginalizing the local population and enhancing their own interests. In Uganda, where Indians were first brought by the British to work on the railway lines, they were accused of taking the livelihood away from the black people and not contributing to the national coffers. Indians were repressed during the brutal regime of Uganda's Idi Amin. They were also evicted in large numbers from Kenya during this time.

The third stage of migration commenced after World War II and brought Hindus first to Britain, where they worked in the labor-hungry British industries. They were soon joined by doctors, businessmen, and other professionals. In the United States, the migration of professionals began in the latter half of the 20th century, which was followed by waves and waves of migration of software professionals. The phenomenon of "twice migration" happened during this phase, with Caribbean Hindus moving to Miami, London, or New York and Kenyan and Ugandan Hindus moving to Britain owing to policies that favored indigenous populations.

In the United States, Indians have done particularly well and their affluence is pronounced. Motels have become synonyms with Patels. Although Indians comprise less than 0.5 percent of the population, no group (excepting the Japanese and Jews) has a higher per capita income than the Indians. It was also in the United States that Indians became targets of racial attacks for the first time. The Hindu woman, clad in a sari and wearing a bindi (vermillion dot) on her forehead, was the focus of attack by the so-called "dot-busters," a New Jersey-based gang of white teenagers who were already responsible for several violent crimes against Indians.

Today you can find several generations of Hindus living overseas. Outside South Asia, Indonesia has the most number of Hindus living abroad (5.9 million) followed by the United States (2 million), South Africa (1.4 million), the United Kingdom (1.3 million), and Malaysia (1.2 million). Among the highest concentrations (i.e., percentage of total population) of Hindus outside South Asia, as per 2002 estimates, Mauritius tops the list (more than 50 percent) followed by Fiji and Guyana (more than 30 percent).

How do Hindus keep in touch with their roots? Despite being away from India for many generations, many Hindus maintain links with the motherland through Bollywood movies, cricket, Indian dances, and arranged marriages.

18

Namaste

Boarding pass in hand, I follow the narrow air bridge leading to the plane. This is my first trip to India after a long time. I am greeted by an air hostess wrapped in a sari and wearing a bindi on her forehead. With a light bow of the head and palms pressed together, she welcomes each passenger with a "Namaste." I have another twelve hours to reach home, but I feel at home already.

Although sari and bindi are distinctive symbols of Indian culture, Namaste is the icon of India in the West, next only to yoga. It is the traditional Indian greeting, whether you are on the street, at home, or on the phone. The word Namaste comes from Sanskrit and literally means "I bow to you." Namaste can be used casually or formally, though it acknowledges that the real meeting is the meeting of minds.

The rest of the world may greet by hugging each other, kissing one another on the cheek, rubbing noses, or bowing gently. The mountain people of Tibet are known to stick out their tongues at each other while greeting. Most of the Western world, however, uses the handshake. I prefer the handshake, for it brings warmth and a personal touch to the meeting. That said, sometimes my hands are slightly wet or smeared in grease after an introduction. And once in a while, I stumble upon one of those tattooed, macho guys who almost crack your wrist bones. Then, of course, we have the fully attired business professional, who will read all sorts of meaning into the very style of your handshake.

Namaste

It is believed the handshake evolved in medieval Europe during the time of knights, who often approached opponents with concealed weapons. A display of an open and empty hand then was a gesture that said, "See, I am unarmed. You can allow me to approach you." No one knows much about the origins of Namaste. While the handshake evolved into a gesture of trust, Namaste had an element of spirituality. It accepts all souls are divine and it reminds us that we can see God in every human being we meet. Namaste is both a mantra (spoken greeting) and a mudra (gesture).

Unlike the Namaste, the handshake has a physical side to it. The opening grip is symbolic of the outgoing, forceful, and materialistic culture of the West. Kings never shake hands with their subjects. Saints do not shake hands with their followers. Namaste, on the other hand, has an unmistakable spiritual reverence to it. It is symbolic of the East, where the inner quality is valued more than your outer worldly possessions. Saints do Namaste. Kings do Namaste.

While the handshake brings intimacy, the Namaste conveys aloofness and humility. It draws you inward, keeping you close to your intuitive nature. A handshake is always between two people, whereas a Namaste can greet an entire legion in one act, something unthinkable of a handshake.

19

The Nature of God

Having listened to people describe Hinduism, I have concluded that most outsiders can be described as illiterates, some as literates, and a very few, the learned. Maybe I'm being harsh to call people illiterates even though they can read and write, but these are the ones who are the loudest in the room and drown out dissenting opinions. Found in every nook and cranny of the Western world, the illiterates have determined without the slightest doubt that Hinduism is polytheistic or the worship of many gods, smugly contending to themselves that multiple gods must be primitive and false.

Next we have the literates, the types that have read about the religion but are overwhelmed by its diversity. They have seen the existence of many gods: a Shakta Hindu adoring Devi, a Saivaite praying to Shiva, a Vaishnava revering Vishnu, and a Smarta Hindu worshiping a chosen god from a pantheon of deities. They have also seen the existence of minor gods, like Hanuman and Ganesha, having both human and animal features. Yet they realize all these gods are manifestations of the one and only god called Brahman. Educated and smart, they will vouch Hinduism is monotheistic.

Then I occasionally run into a few of those learned types, who live in a world of slokas and mantras, yet always have a powerful message to hand down from time to time. Such is the vastness and diversity of the religion that, after speaking with them, I am convinced it will take me a heavenly day to fully comprehend the religion. The learned ones call Hinduism a henotheistic religion, meaning the worship of one supreme god without denying the existence of others. When it comes to describing Hinduism in a nutshell, the learned ones are spot on. That's exactly the nature of Hinduism with its diversity, yet never denying the existence of other paths to god.

The learned types have also taught me Hinduism is panentheism in nature. It's an ultra-long word, but I understand it means god is both immanent (within) and transcendent (beyond). In other words, god is not only residing within all things, but beyond our conception of the world. This is different from pantheism (where god is the natural world, i.e., immanent, not transcendent) and traditional theism (Christianity) where god is above the world, but not within us (transcendent, but not immanent).

From the learned types, I came to know that the only deity worshiped by Hindus of all denominations is Ganesha, the elephant God. By the way, in case you are wondering, a heavenly day is actually one day in the life of Brahma and consists of 4.32 billion years. Such incredibly long days, you may say. Hang in there my friend, for it's gonna be one hell of a ride understanding Hinduism.

> *The illiterate of the 21st century will not be those who cannot read and write, but those who cannot learn, unlearn, and relearn.*
> – Alvin Toffler (1928–)

20

The Odd Jodi

Jodi, meaning pair, is not in the English language yet, but it's a popular word found in most Indian languages. To me, the Hindu religion and the English language are the odd Jodi. I know one is a religion, and the other a language, but if you trace the evolution of the English language, you will notice a striking similarity with that of Hinduism.

During the colonization of ancient India, the British endeavored to understand Hinduism in order to govern the country and establish a relationship with the people. For Hinduism, it was through English that it reached out to the West, particularly through the works of Swami Vivekananda in the 19th century. Both are third in their categories; Hinduism, the third-largest religion, and English, the third-largest native language. Both don't have a central authority to manage their affairs. English does not have France's Académie Française and Hinduism doesn't have the Catholic Church's Pope. Both have variations in them. Hinduism is a multi-traditional religion while English has many varieties, including British, American, and Australian. Yet not one variation in either Hinduism or English is considered the pukka religion or the standard language.

If Hinduism is the all-accepting religion, then English is the all-accepting language. Anything goes in either Hinduism or English. Both have been receptive to new ideas and continuously adapted and evolved over the years. You can find many linguistic borrowings in English and the list of loan words continues to grow. Likewise, you will find both centuries-old concepts and terms of recent vintage in Hinduism. The word "Hinduism" is only about 300 years old, even though the religion is more than five thousand years old. The concept of Maya was introduced in the 6th century, while ahimsa was popularized by Gandhi in the 20th century.

Fascinating so far? We'll continue the journey another time over a variation of English called Inglish.

CONCEPTS

Whoever undertakes to set himself up as a judge of Truth and Knowledge is shipwrecked by the laughter of the gods.
— Albert Einstein (1879-1955)

21

Many Many Many Gods

> *India has two million gods, and worships them all. In religion all other countries are paupers; India is the only millionaire.*
> – Mark Twain

For every person who is appreciative of the ancient Hindu wisdom, you can be sure there's one who is apprehensive of its beliefs and customs. Although Hinduism is a mixture of some old traditions and cultures, the one that bewilders most people is the astounding number of gods displayed in paintings, sculpture, and other forms of art. Soon it dawns upon them that the many gods and goddesses are merely manifestations of the single supreme spirit called Brahman. When it comes to Hinduism, you see, first impressions can almost always be wrong. Yet there's always a dimwit who will sleep through the journey of discovering Hinduism and then loudly proclaim, "Oh! My God! So many, many, many gods!" I know it is harsh to call him a fool, but he might do nicely until a real fool comes along.

In spiritual terms, Hinduism is a religion that is both immanent and transcendent. Immanence means god is present in everything. For Hindus, man is not cut off from the divine, for they believe god is omnipresent. The part of god present in all beings is called Atman. We are individually little drops of the ocean and collectively we form the ocean. In the Biblical tradition, man is not immanent, except in the instance where God became immanent through Jesus Christ. Transcendence, on the other hand, is a state that is beyond the limits of all possible experience. For Hindus, Brahman is transcendent and can be experienced by a person by bringing his mind progressively to the highest state of consciousness.

So when people talk about millions of gods, what are they really saying? There's only one supreme reality or god in Hinduism, and that invisible spirit is called Brahman. The misunderstanding, however, stems from their inability to distinguish between Nirguna Brahman and Saguna Brahman.

Hindus refer to the transcendental state of the supreme spirit as Nirguna Brahman. In this state, God is genderless, eternal, infinite, and changeless. It cannot assume a personality, for attaching a personality becomes a limitation. Hindus also use expressions like Absolute Reality, Ultimate Reality, Consciousness, and Infinite Bliss to describe Nirguna Brahman. The great Hindu saint and philosopher Shankaracharya referred to God as "Satchidanandam," meaning Brahman is eternal, consciousness, and bliss.

Nirguna Brahman is formless and changeless, but the human mind has difficulty visualizing Nirguna Brahman, because the mind is incapable of thinking other than in human terms. So we resort to metaphors in the language, and these metaphors unwittingly project human attributes in Nirguna Brahman. The impersonal Brahman then acquires a human-like personality called Saguna Brahman or Ishwara. Hindus look up to Ishwara as a father, mother, friend, child, husband, or even a lover, for such relationships establish a personal connection with god. Many saints of Hinduism such as Kamalakanta, Ramprasad, and Ramakrishna Paramahamsa have looked upon Ishwara as the divine mother.

Over the years, many personal gods were born, and along with them stories and myths. Passed along by word of mouth, these stories and legends became great epics with wisdom and insight. And thousands of years of singing and chanting and weaving together stories of reality with stories of fantasy became what is Hinduism today. Vishnu and Shiva and Krishna and Rama are all different forms of Saguna Brahman and all point to the supreme spirit, Nirguna Brahman.

Next time someone takes you to the corner of a room and whispers in your ear that Hindus have 330 million gods, pinch him in the arm, slap him in the face, or shake him by his shoulders. You can rarely change a fool, but you can remind him of one, occasionally.

22

Sanatana Dharma

> *Sanatana means Eternal. In its purest form, this religion is Sanatana, because it is based on Truth. Truth is immortal and is never annihilated. It remains the same yesterday, today and forever.*
>
> – Swami Rama Tirtha (1873–1906)

The author Andrew Harvey, in his book *Teachings of the Hindu Mystics*, refers to an incident where an evangelical missionary persuades an old sage of Calcutta to convert to Christianity. The missionary, with carefully rehearsed moves and in animated tones, waves, weeps, shudders, shakes his head, and ecstatically evokes the joys of paradise. The sage listens intently without uttering a word. As the missionary goes in for the close, the sage slowly starts to speak. "I accept wholeheartedly, dear honored Sir, that Jesus Christ was indeed a very divine master whose life and teachings are of permanent sacred value to humanity. But the Buddha was also such a divine master, and so, may I add, was my dear Swami, Sri Ramakrishna [Paramahamsa]. Why would God, after all, be so mean as to give humanity only one divine master and that one only for the white people?"

With a slew of divine masters chronicled in its timeless history, Hinduism is not a religion in the conventional sense, for it is not based on the words of a founding father. Most people consider Hinduism both a philosophy and a religion with a blurry line separating the two. Coming from one of the oldest civilizations of the world, Hinduism brings with it a rich set of traditions and ideas from its ancestral past. Over the years many conflicting beliefs and practices also developed side by side. Among these myriads of thoughts and philosophies, a few core beliefs and attitudes bind Hinduism together and lend it its distinctive character.

The term "Hinduism" is of recent vintage, coined less than 300 years ago. The original term used to address the religious tradition of India was "Sanatana Dharma." From Sanskrit, this translates to eternal religion and is based on the natural laws that govern the cosmos. Sanatana Dharma is the path that leads to the discovery of truth by living in harmony with cosmic law. The principles of Santana Dharma were codified in the Vedas more than six thousand years ago, but Hindus consider them eternal with a special significance. The world comes and goes, but the laws governing Santana Dharma remain true beyond time and space.

Abrahamic religions believe that the world originated around 4000 BCE and will come to an end in the future when God establishes us at eternity. Each of these religions also believes that it provides the surest path to salvation. For the Hindus, the world is not just thousands of years old, but billions of years old. Furthermore they believe the universe in which our world belongs will die, be reborn and die again, in an endless cycle. Just as day follows night in perpetual rhythm, so does birth follow death, as the entire universe undergoes cycles of birth, death, and rebirth.

"In each beginning of the world, Vishnu is lying asleep on an ocean of milk on the back of a cobra called Ananta-Sesha whose numerous hoods form a canopy. In the course of Vishnu's dream, a lotus grows out of his navel, and in the petals is a shiny golden egg. This egg will hatch into our solar system under the guidance of Brahma, who is the mastermind of our local universe, including the Sun and Moon.

...

The lifetime of Brahma is 100 heavenly years with each day equivalent to 4.32 billion human years. Shiva's drumbeat marks the end of Brahma and our world. At the end, everything in this solar system is dissolved, including Brahma himself. This is followed by one hundred kalpas of chaos, after which another Brahma is born and a new cycle begins."

During each cycle, as the world comes into existence, many religions spring forth in many parts of the world. And as the world fades into nonexistence, these religions fade into obscurity. While Hindus proudly call their religion eternal, the sages of ancient India were equally convinced that there are many ways to seek the truth. "All paths lead to me," says Krishna in the Bhagavad Gita.

I call myself a Sanatani Hindu, because I believe in the Vedas, the Upanishads, the Puranas, and all that goes by the name of Hindu scripture, and therefore in avataras [reincarnation] and rebirth; I believe in the varnashrama dharma in a sense, in my opinion strictly Vedic but not in its presently popular crude sense; I believe in the protection of cow ... I do not disbelieve in murti pooja [idol worship].

– Mahatma Gandhi (1869–1948)

23

The Scriptures of Hinduism

Walk into any bookstore or library in the West, and you will be hard-pressed to find a handful of books on Hinduism. It seems the world's oldest religion has little to offer in terms of literature. But nothing can be further from the truth. Hindu literature is so vast and diverse that there's enough material to fill up every aisle and shelf of the central library, the sub-libraries and the branch libraries. Most Western libraries, however, stock a shelf or two of popular Hindu texts.

Which ones? Or what are the holy books of Hinduism? Although Hinduism does not have a single authoritative scripture, most orthodox Hindus regard the Vedas as the holy book.

Hindus believe the Vedas existed before the beginning of time and were revealed to ancient sages in their meditative trances. Most scholars, however, place their origins around 2500 BCE, although evidence points to an even earlier existence. For thousands of years, the Vedas were transmitted orally and memorization was the only way to learn them until they were written down about 800 BCE. The revealed texts of Vedas belong to a category of scriptures called "shruti," meaning "heard." There is another category of Hindu scripture called "smriti," meaning "remembered," which was perceived by the recollection of historical events by well-known authorities. The shruti texts form the final authority in Hinduism. The smriti texts are also revered but second to the Vedas. The Hindu epics Mahabharata and Ramayana belong to the smriti category.

What we call the Vedas actually consist of four books (Rig Veda, Sama Veda, Yajur Veda, and Atharva Veda) and their philosophical compendiums (Aranyakas and Upanishads). The most important among these works is the Rig Veda, which is a collection of 1,017 hymns. Each of the four books is further divided into two sections: Samhita and Brahmana. While Samhitas contain the hymns, Brahmanas provide explanation for the hymns and procedures for conducting rituals. The philosophical sections known as Aranyakas (forest-treatises) and Upanishads (secret teachings) are meant for those engaged in spiritual practices and mystical insights. Both these texts discuss the inner significance of the Vedic rites. The Upanishads, numbering 108, hold an important place in Hinduism and are particularly well-known for their profundities.

Besides the epics, the smriti literature also includes eighteen Puranas and numerous law books. The Puranas are specially created works that break down the complexity of Hindu scriptures and present the deeper truths in parables and easy-to-understand language. Smriti also contain law books called Dharma Shastras that are authored by ancient sages like Yajnavalkya, Vasishta, and Gautama. These law books are manuals of codes of conduct for the Hindus, and do not pertain to any particular legal system.

Among the Dharma Shastras, Manu-smriti, the law book of Manu, is the most well-known. Closely related to the Dharma Shastra is the Artha Shastra, which deals with statecraft and economic policy, and Niti Shastra, which contains the famous fables of Panchatantra and Hitopadesha. The Dharma Shastras, along with the Artha Shastras, form the codes of Hindu law, parallel to the Muslim Sharia or the Jewish Talmud.

Although most Hindu literature falls under shruti and smriti, there are others like Darshanas that do not fall under any category. The Darshanas correspond to the six philosophical schools of thought (Sankhya, Purva Mimamsa, Vedanta, Yoga, Nyaya, and Vaisheshika) and have their foundation in the Vedas.

Closely paralleling the Vedic disciplines, Hinduism has another set of shruti texts called Agamas. While the Vedas relate to every Hindu, the Agamas apply specifically to the different denominations within Hinduism, such as Saivism, Shaktism and Vaishnavism. The Agamas comprise revelations on yoga, mantra, tantra, kundalini and many others. While many Agamas have been published, most still remain inaccessible and are protected by families and guilds. Among the published one, there are ninety-two Saiva Agamas, seventy-seven Shakta Agamas and 108 Vaishnava Agamas.

Both Vedas and Agamas have ancillary texts. The ancillary texts of Vedas are the Vedangas and Upavedas, while those of Agamas are called Upagamas and Paddhatis. Popular among these supplementary works include Jyotisha (astrology), Ayurveda (medicine), Gandharvaveda (music and arts), and Kama Sutras (erotic pleasures).

This is a sampling of the holy Hindu books. If you think the volume of Hindu literature is huge, you are mistaken. They are massive and may take several cycles of rebirths to master ☺.

> *The average Hindu knows more about the rituals but less about the religion than he realizes.*
>
> – Swami Achuthananda

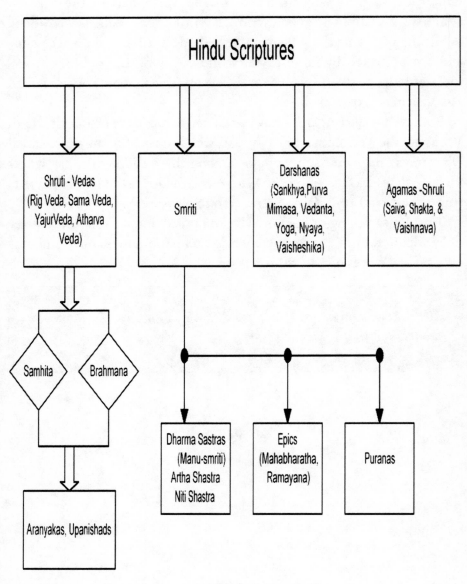

Hindu Scriptures

Shruti - Vedas
(Rig Veda, Sama Veda, YajurVeda, Atharva Veda)

Smriti

Darshanas
(Sankhya,Purva Mimasa, Vedanta, Yoga, Nyaya, Vaisheshika)

Agamas -Shruti
(Saiva, Shakta, & Vaishnava)

Samhita

Brahmana

Aranyakas, Upanishads

Dharma Sastras
(Manu-smriti)
Artha Shastra
Niti Shastra

Epics
(Mahabharatha, Ramayana)

Puranas

Scriptures of Hinduism

24

The Vedas

Outsiders beginning to understand Hinduism are often fascinated with one distinguishing aspect of the religion: the presence of elaborate rituals that occupy a central part of the religion. Rituals vary from place to place, but it's a little-known fact that the most sacred ones, such as the daily prayers of a Brahmin or the sacraments accompanying birth, death, and marriage, make use of the same Vedic verses as those used some five thousand years ago. Although the ability of Brahmin priests to preserve the Vedic verses verbatim over centuries has been astounding, Hindus find nothing unusual about it. Preserving the word of the Vedas is the dharma or religious duty of the Brahmins.

In Sanskrit "Veda" means knowledge. The Vedas constitute not only the oldest sacred texts of Hinduism but also the most revered of the scriptures. In pictures, Brahma and Vishnu are often seen holding a book or pustaka containing the Vedas in one of their many hands. The criterion for orthodoxy in Hinduism is the acceptance of the Vedas. The Hindu schools of thought that accept the authority of the Vedas are called "astika," meaning "it is" people, while those that don't are called "nastika" or "it is not" people. While the darshanas or the six Hindu philosophical schools belong to the astik traditions, Buddhism and Jainism are nastik traditions that openly reject the teachings of the Vedas.

Hindus do not believe that the Vedas were conceived by a group of authors. Rather it is believed that the Vedic verses were communicated at higher states of meditation to the rishis (sages) of ancient India, whose names appear in the texts. Some hymns appear to be written by women poets, for the names Ghosa, Apala, and Lopamundra can be seen in early samhitas. The Vedas were then orally passed along to other Brahmins, who were the custodians since the beginning of time. Since writing down the text was considered an act of desecration, the Vedas were transmitted orally for thousands of years.

To preserve the Vedas, the Brahmin priests used a variety of techniques. They memorized the verses of Vedas both backwards and forwards. They also memorized the verses in other combinations, such as skipping alternate words and used memorization aids, such as chanting the Vedas to certain rhythms and moving hands according to certain rules. All these ensured that the Vedas were pronounced exactly like they were thousands of years ago with little or no loss of syllable until they were finally written down around 800 BCE. First written in the archaic language of Vedic Sanskrit, the Vedas nowadays is available in almost all Indian languages and in some European languages.

Although the Vedas is divided into four major collections (Rig Veda, Yajur Veda, Sama Veda and Atharva Veda), when Hindus speak of the Vedas, they mean the whole corpus, starting with the Vedic hymns (Samhitas), the ritual treatise (Brahmanas), the theologies (Aranyakas), and the philosophical section (Upanishads). The West has often used the Vedas to apply only to the hymns (Samhita) portion of each collection.

You will be surprised to learn that the Vedas are nothing like the religious texts of the Bible or the Koran. The compositions are largely in the form of poetry or rhythmic prose composed with great economy of expression. The hymns are couched in simple language but address some highly philosophical concepts that raise more questions than answers. For instance, in the creation hymn, known as the Nasadiya, there is a speculation on the origin of the universe. The hymn leaves the question hanging and concludes that perhaps no one knew how it all came to be.

In the beginning there was neither non-existence nor existence then;
There was neither the realm of space nor the sky which is beyond.
What stirred? In whose protection?
Was there water, bottomlessly deep?

There was neither death nor immortality then.
There was no distinguishing sign of night nor of day.
That one breathed, windless, but its own impulse.
Other than that there was nothing beyond.

The interpretation[9] of the Vedas has not been static over the years. Many hymns, particularly contained in the Rig Veda, are obscure or paradoxical in their meaning that more has been read in them than what is actually said. It appears that every generation has uniquely interpreted the Vedic verses in a manner befitting that generation. Most Vedic hymns are framed as riddles, but they are also offerings of great beauty and artistry.

Although the Vedas are the most sacred, you are unlikely to find a copy of the Vedas at Hindu homes or kept on the bedside table of Indian hotels. Most Hindus know a few hymns, which they recite regularly at temple and home liturgies. The Vedas are particularly significant to the Brahmins, the highest caste of the society and the custodians of the scripture.

The Vedic hymns are addressed to many gods like Indra, Agni, Varuna, and Rudra. Interestingly, despite the slew of gods that appear in Hinduism, the Vedas have recognized the notion of a single god right from the beginning. The Yajur Veda identifies this single supreme power that reveals itself into many forms as Prajapati, the lord of creatures, in the following text.

Agni is That, Vayu is That, Chandramas is That,
Light is That, Brahman is That, Waters are Those, Prajapati is He!

One dominant feature of Vedic religious life was the ritual sacrifice called yagna, a practice that continues even today although in a milder form. The ritual sacrifices are performed with a fire and are conducted by ritual specialists and priests, who supervise the making of altars and recitation of hymns.

Also in the Vedas, you will find the first mention of four classes of society that would blight Hinduism forever.

---

9 As interpreted by Wendy Doniger.

From his mouth came the priestly class
from his arms, the rulers,
the producers came from his legs;
from his feet came the servant class.

Although the origins of what eventually came to be called the caste system (varna) are generally seen to lie in these verses from the Rig Veda, it is likely that the classification of society had already taken place long before its composition.

It has been said that the verses of the Vedas have never been matched in their profundity. The Vedas symbolized not only the dawn of Hinduism, but also the pinnacle of Indian philosophy and human wisdom.

25

The Vedic Pantheon

Look up at the sky, and you'll see a huge, flaming ball of gas containing hydrogen and helium surrounded by vast emptiness. When the ancients of the Vedic age looked up, they saw something different. Where we saw fact and science and no meaning, they found the sky as a magical place, bubbling with life, full of gods and demons, each with their own myths, stories, and symbols.

It is early morning at the kingdom of Vedas. Ushas, the goddess of dawn, has put on her embroidered garments. Creating light for the world of life, she stirs all creatures from their sleep. The Vedic dance has begun. The drumbeat of the morning sun greets the arrival of Indra, the ruler of the heavens and the vanquisher of the demon Vritra, riding a white elephant and wielding the dazzling weapon of lightning called Vajra. At times scheming and at times troubled, Indra lives more like an earthly king than a heavenly lord, particularly on occasions when, after consuming Soma, the sacrificial ambrosia of immortality, he loses control and makes a royal fool of himself.

Standing beside Indra is the god Rudra, the militant god of storms and lightning. Although not in the same league as Indra, the fierce Rudra enjoys a unique position in the Vedic pantheon because of his tempestuous nature. From afar, the rumblings of a chariot can be heard. Coming toward them is the sun god Surya seated on a triumphal chariot driven by seven horses and holding a lotus in his hand. Surya is sometimes mentioned as the creator of the universe, and his children are Yama and Yami.

As you may have guessed, Indra, Ushas, Rudra, and Surya were some of the principal gods during the Vedic age. Another principal deity was Agni, often invoked with Indra because of his fondness for the Soma drink. The sacrificial fire was an important religious practice, and Agni, depicted with two heads with seven fiery tongues in each head, was the embodiment of fire. Agni is also represented as a messenger between humankind and gods since he delivers the sacrificial offerings that ascend as smoke to the heavens.

Mitra is the deity for honesty and friendship, and, along with his brother Varuna, oversees the natural systems that govern life. They are the custodians of the sacred Vedic laws. Among the other popular deities, Yama is the god of death and together with his female counterpart Yami, represent the first human beings. Yama, in fact, is the first man who experienced death.

The Vedic seers had tremendous capacity for imagination and enchantment. For us Agni is the chemical process of carbonization, but for the Vedic people, Agni was a deva taking the persona of fire. The Vedic world was spiritually alive and kicking. The power of the spirit overshadowed everything else.

You will be surprised to know that the Vedic dance ended long back. Few Hindus worship the Vedic Gods anymore. More popular deities have replaced them over the years. Indra is no longer the king, and Mitra and Varuna exist only as names. Rudra has been sidelined for Shiva. Vishnu, who played a cameo in the Vedas as the sun god, rose to prominence in later texts. The newer pantheon is centered upon the three main gods, Brahma, Vishnu, and Shiva, with their consorts or shaktis.

> *In religious publishing, Christianity has a plethora of authors and their books that explore the religion in excruciating detail. Buddhism has Dalai Lama and his perennial hits about the philosophy of life. Hinduism has voluminous, hard-to-comprehend textbooks written by esteemed professors of eastern religions for the benefit of other professors of eastern religions.*
>
> – Swami Achuthananda

26

Om – The Sound of the Cosmos

Modern science and ancient Hindu teachings agree on one thing: matter is made up of vibrating energy. Ordinary audible sounds are created when two or more elements strike at each other, like the sound produced when the wind rustles the leaves or when the bow slides over the violin strings or when the waves splash across the shores. Ancient India had discovered another awesome sound caused by elements vibrating together. Referred to as "anahata nada" in Sanskrit, the unstruck sound most resembles the sound of the primal energy and is called Om.

Held in high respect, Om is a word that basically says nothing. No one really knows about the exact origin of Om, but every Hindu knows it when they see or hear it. As a symbol, the Om is to Hindus what the cross is to Christians, or the menorah is to Jews. It is the oldest mantra known to the sages of India and the most sacred. Found by itself on most letterheads, pendants, and wedding cards, Om also occurs in everyday prayers like "Om Shanti Om" and "Om Namo Narayana." It is enshrined in every Hindu temple and family shrine.

Om, the sound, stands for cosmic vibration, which is like the drone of millions of bees humming together in chorus. Scientists have found that the cosmic sound cannot be heard by man's naked ears, for the vibrations emanating from planets are pitched twenty octaves below man's hearing. However, Hindus believe the unheard cosmic sounds are audible to spiritual practitioners in the higher state of consciousness.

The sound Om is also called Pranava in Sanskrit, meaning one that sustains life and runs through our breath or prana.

Om, the symbol, however, is identified with Brahman, the Absolute Reality, from which everything evolved, according to Hinduism. It is believed that repeated utterance of Om identifies oneself with the cosmic resonance, thereby reentering the source from which one emerged. Hindu tradition has it that this ancient mantra is composed of three sounds: A, U, M, and concluded by silence. These are symbolically related to the basic states of consciousness, which are waking, dreaming, and sleeping. The fourth state or silence is the highest state and is a way of concentrating on, or even merging with, the absolute.

Om embodies the most profound concepts of Hindu belief and most religious Hindus begin their day by uttering the word. A newborn child is ushered into the world with this holy sign. Om is also initiated into the life of a Hindu and remains with him forever, as the symbol of piety.

Om is also a popular symbol in contemporary body art and tattoos. Many Western rock bands have used it in their works, including George Harrison, who used the symbol Om as the 3 on the cover of his album "Thiry Three and 1/3." The symbol is used in almost every page as a header in this book.

Om

Om Shanti Om

27

Veda Vyasa

The government of India confers the highest honor for achievement by awarding a two-inch-long ribbon attached to a pipal-shaped leaf carrying the inscription "Bharat Ratna." Considered the most prestigious of the awards, the Bharat Ratna or "Jewel of India" is bestowed upon truly inspirational heroes, and the list of recipients includes Ravi Shankar and Indira Gandhi. Also included are a few non-Indians like Nelson Mandela and a lady by the name Agnes Gonxha Bojaxhiu, popularly known as Mother Teresa. I am afraid Veda Vyasa is not in the list, but that's okay.

Although Bharat Ratna was established shortly after India's independence in 1947, Hinduism from time immemorial had recognized outstanding achievers by bestowing upon them the fountain of longevity or "chiranjeevi." The Hindu scriptures identify seven such chiranjeevis. While each of the chiranjeevis is qualified in his own special way, when it comes to literature, none can surpass the skill and mastery of Vyasa, for he is believed to be the greatest seer, guru, author, poet, and philosopher the Hindu religion has ever seen.

Krishna Dvaipayana, who later came to be known as Veda Vyasa, was born some 3500 years ago to an illustrious family of sages. Son of eminent sage Parasara, the author of Vishnu Puranam, and the great grandson of the famous sage Vasishta, Vyasa was believed to be a genius by birth and was initiated into the study of sacred lore at an early age. The greatest achievement of Vyasa was the monumental task of classifying the primordial single Veda into four, as was then required for different classes of priests. So profound was this effort that a grateful generation honored him with the title Veda Vyasa or the "splitter of the Vedas."

Vyasa is more popularly known as the author of Mahabharata in which he colorfully narrates the wisdom of Vedas through tales of sages and kings. Vyasa himself appears as an important character in this epic. The Mahabharata is four times the length of the Bible and eight times the length of Homer's *Iliad* and *Odyssey* combined, and this treasure trove of worldly wisdom, containing the Bhagavad Gita, is often described as the fifth Veda.

From his home in Badari Ashram, located in the mountains of Himalayas, Vyasa wrote the Brahma Sutras (Vedanta Sutras) or pithy aphorisms that crystallize the essence of Vedas, particularly the Upanishads. The Brahma Sutras are organized into four chapters and contain 564 sutras. The sutras have been the subject of many philosophers of Hindu schools of thought, who have written lengthy commentaries about them. Vyasa is also credited with writing the eighteen Puranas of which Bhagavata Purana, focusing on Lord Krishna's childhood, is the most popular. The Puranas, totaling about 400,000 verses, are religious scriptures that expound the teachings of Vedas using stories and legends. Although Puranas are mostly devotions to god, they also include subjects like cosmology, astrology, and Ayurveda.

Not much is known about the life of Vyasa other than from these works. Vyasa accomplished through his works in his lifetime what most men achieve in a dozen lifetimes. Such has been the volume of intellectual output that it has been debated whether Vyasa was a single person or a class of scholars who went by the same name. It has been said that what has not been touched by his intellect has never been found elsewhere.

Vyasa has long gone, leaving his immortal works to the world, but to the Hindus, Vyasa continues to live in Badari Ashram as a chiranjeevi with an intellect beyond the reach of ordinary people. Every year on the day of Guru Purnima (July-August), Hindus celebrate his birthday.

> *Only a life lived for others is worth living.*
> – Albert Einstein (1879–1955)

28

The Upanishads

Composed between 800–300 BCE and considered the crown jewels of the Vedas, the Upanishads marked the birth of Indian philosophy, becoming the main source of inspiration for philosophical thinking for thousands of years. The term "Upanishad" literally means "to sit near," denoting wisdom transmitted by gurus to select students in accordance with the teacher-student or guru-shishya tradition.

However devoted, every thinking person will be confronted with pangs of religious doubt at some point in his life. Although the Vedic Samhitas and Brahmanas are excellent manuals on rituals to worship God, none answered the philosophical questions of life many were seeking. The writings of the Upanishads were developed primarily as a reaction against the divine status of the Vedas and the elaborate ritualism of the Brahmin priests, who have been sole custodians of the sacred scriptures. Many teachings reflect this opposition in no uncertain terms. The Mundaka Upanishad, for instance, states that "whoever hopes for real good to accrue from these rites is a fool and is sure to be overtaken again by death and decrepitude." Interestingly the Upanishads do not completely reject the early hymns and sacrificial rituals, but rather reinterpret the material in a different light. They show some continuity with the earlier Vedic text and were therefore included as part of the Vedas.

You will be surprised to learn that the Upanishads are not modern-style philosophical textbooks. On the contrary, key ideas are developed using parables or metaphors and appear to be loosely organized. They are mostly written as conversations between a teacher and student, a husband and wife, or a fellow philosopher and another, with some texts scattered in many places. Although the Upanishads were composed by many, the main figure is believed to be Yajnavalkya, the great sage who propounded the doctrine of "neti-neti" (not this, not this), an analytical process of conceptualizing Brahman by defining what it is not. Many earlier Vedic teachers like Manu, Brihaspati, Ayasya, and Narada are also found in the Upanishads.

Among the 200 Upanishads of various lengths, 108 are recognized as sacred, with eleven of these texts considered particularly important. These are Aitareya, Mandukya, Brihadaranyaka, Mundaka, Chandogya, Prashna, Isha, Shvetashvatara, Katha, Taittiriya, and Kena Upanishads.

The Upanishads in general strive to address "brahmavidya" or supreme science, which seeks knowledge not of the external world but of the hidden reality that underpins this world. The central teachings of Hinduism, such as the concepts of karma (action), samsara (reincarnation), moksha (liberation), and Atman are found in the Upanishads. It is also in the Upanishads that the concept of Brahman gets fully developed, an idea that went a long way towards unifying Hinduism. While the nature gods like Indra, Agni, Vayu, and Surya were subordinated to Prajapati in the Vedas, Prajapati, in turn, was subordinated to Brahman in the Upanishads. The Upanishads also identify a path, known as jnana (knowledge) yoga, to attain moksha and thereby achieving liberation from the cycle of rebirths. (Note that the Bhagavad Gita's path to moksha was based on karma yoga or detached action focused on God.)

Unlike in the West, philosophy and religion never got separated in India. Philosophical reflection is still an important part of understanding Hinduism. Although the basic philosophical ideas of the Upanishads led to the creation of several Hindu darshanas or schools of thought, the Upanishads as such have become detached from any specific school of thought and have been adopted as standard teaching by Brahmins and other classes.

The Upanishads have been described by Aurobindo as the supreme work of the Indian mind. The significance of the Upanishads has been acknowledged by writers and scholars like Schopenhauer, Emerson, and Thoreau. The collection is also listed in *100 Most Influential Books Ever Written*, compiled in 1998 by British poet Martin Seymour-Smith. Because the Upanishads are the last text in the Vedas, they are often referred to as "Vedanta,"[10] meaning the end of Veda.

---

10 The term Vedanta also refers to a school of thought (which includes Shankara's Advaita) in which the Upanishads play a prominent but not exclusive role.

29

The Hindu Cosmogony - I

In the beginning there was nothing but emptiness. Then God created the world. For the Abrahamic (Judeo-Christian-Islamic) religions, the universe came into existence around 4000 BCE. According to them, the universe will move forward and come to an end on the Day of Judgment.

To modern science, the world is not merely thousands but billions of years old. That our planet is only six thousand years old is incredibly too short. As the theory of evolution goes, even monkeys took about twenty-five million years to shed their tails and turn into apes, our ancestors.

Regardless of your beliefs, the origin of the universe has vexed mankind from time immemorial. Every major religion has formulated a theory that explains the beginning of the world, but nothing is incredibly stunning and closer to the modern scientific view than the ancient Hindu version. It makes the Western version of creation look like a movie running in fast forward.

Western religions believe time is linear (begin-go-end), but Hindus believe time is cyclical. The cycle is repeating and without end. Duration is in billions of years instead of thousands. There is no permanent end for the universe, for the end leads to a new beginning. Thus every billions of years, the universe comes into existence, disappears, and the cycle continues ad infinitum.

In Hinduism, time is calculated in yugas. There are four yugas.

Kali Yuga	432,000 years
Dvapara Yuga	864,000 years (2 x Kali Yuga)
Treta Yuga	1,296,000 years (3 x Kali Yuga)
Satya Yuga	1,728, 000 years (4 x Kali Yuga)

One complete cycle involving the four yugas is called a maha-yuga, which has 4,320,000 years. A maha-yuga starts with the longest Satya yuga, followed by Treta, Dvapara, and finally Kali. Things such as spirituality, morality, and longevity turn from best to worst as we move along the yugas in a maha-yuga. The Satya yuga gets afforded the best of times in spirituality and morality. The longevity of a human being in the Satya Yuga is supposedly one hundred thousand years. (The Mahabharata and the Puranas are replete with characters living for several thousands of years.) The quality of life deteriorates further in the Treta and Dvapara Yugas and is the worst in the Kali Yuga, which Hindus call the age of degeneration. It is believed the Hindu god Rama appeared during the Treta Yuga, while Krishna was found at the end of Dvapara yuga. Hindus believe we are currently living in Kali Yuga, which started about five thousand years back.

A thousand maha-yugas is called a kalpa; therefore a kalpa is 4,320,000,000 years. According to the Hindu tradition, time moves on in these great cycles, yuga after yuga, kalpa after kalpa, eternally.

In the Hindu view of the origin of the universe, Brahma is the creator of our solar system, and Vishnu is the lord of the galaxy. When Brahma wakes up every day, he creates the three worlds (heavens, middle, and lower regions). At the end of the day, when he goes to sleep, they are reduced to chaos. Those who have not obtained liberation are judged and must prepare for rebirth based on karma when Brahma wakes up the next day. Time is eternal and is a never-ending cycle of creation and destruction, with each complete cycle being represented by one hundred years in the life of Brahma. At the end of this period, everything in this solar system is dissolved, including Brahma himself. This is followed by one hundred years of chaos, after which another Brahma is born and a new cycle begins.

Fascinated with the Hindu theory of creation, Carl Sagan, the American scientist and author, wrote, "The Hindu religion is the only one of the world's great faiths dedicated to the idea that the cosmos itself undergoes an immense, indeed an infinite, number of deaths and rebirths. It is the only religion in which the time scales correspond to those of modern scientific cosmology. Its cycles run from our ordinary day and night to a day and night of Brahma, 8.64 billion years long. Longer than the age of the Earth or the Sun and about half the time since the Big Bang. And there are much longer time scales still."

While the Western religions struggle to square with scientific reality, Hinduism meets science head-on, as new discoveries validate ancient truth. The Hindus may have used primitive expressions and crude mythology to express their thoughts, but the insights of ancient sages—modern scientists overwhelmingly approve—were stunningly incredible compared with the religious traditions of the world.

> *Science without religion is lame, religion without science is blind.*
> – Albert Einstein (1879–1955)

> *To the philosophers of India, however, relativity is no new discovery, just as the concept of light years is no matter for astonishment to people used to thinking of time in millions of kalpas. The fact that the wise men of India have not been concerned with technological applications of this knowledge arises from the circumstance that technology is but one of innumerable ways of applying it.*
> – Alan Watts (1915–1973)

30

The Hindu Cosmogony - II

The might of the Himalayas fades into insignificance when you've seen what I've seen. At about 450,000 kilometers high, Mount Meru is more awesome than the eight-kilometer-tall peaks of the Himalayas. While many lives have been lost attempting to scale the peaks of the Himalayas, Hindus believe that the human journey of life begins at the summit of Mount Meru.

In Hindu mythology, the earth is shaped like a wheel and is the innermost of seven concentric islands separated by seven seas. Central among the islands is Jambu Dwipa, or the island of Jambu tree. (The Jambu is rose apple, a variety of plum found in Asian countries.) At the center of this island lies the golden mountain of Meru, whose summit is the site of Brahma's abode, which is encircled by the River Ganges and surrounded by the cities of Indra and other deities.

Beginning with Brahma's palace, the seven levels below comprise the heavens or Svarka Lokas. The heavens are inhabited by Devas (divine beings in charge of natural phenomena), sages, gandharvas, and a host of other pious beings. It is presided over by Indra, who is the king of heaven.

Below the heavens is situated the earth or Bhurloka. The earth is said to go down to about 400,000 kilometers and consists of seven planes of Patala Lokas occupied by Asuras (human look-alikes who have turned against the path of dharma, acting in enmity to Lord Vishnu), Yakshas, and Dhanavas. Although the Patala Lokas are sometimes referred to as hell, particularly in *Vishnu Purana*, they are not a place for torture or punishment, rather a place for the confinement of those dedicated to materialism. Below the Patala Lokas extend the coils of a dark snake called Ananta-Sesha, on whose thousand heads rest the entire world. The snake coils form the couch on which Vishnu stretches himself in rest.

The real hell or Naraka begins below the earth and the waters and extends to the bottom of the universe. The hell is full of instruments of torture and comprises twenty-eight levels of torture cells into which sinners are cast. Yama, the god of death and punishment, presides over the hells. Chitragupta, his secretary, keeps track of the good and bad deeds of every person during his or her lifetime.

Although Mount Meru dwarfs its rivals in size, you will not find it listed in the *Guinness World Records*. Mount Meru is purely imaginary and was created by the rishis of ancient India. In Hindu mythology, it always remains a sacred mountain, and in an astronomical sense, represents the north-south axis of the earth.

31

Heaven and Hell

I f you do good things you will go to heaven after life, but if you do bad things, you'll head straight to hell. For every major religion, whether you go to heaven or hell depends on how you lead your life in this world. But as a devoted Hindu, please explain why you are perpetuating this myth when there's no place like heaven or hell in Hinduism.

Please don't think I am belittling your beliefs. To be sure, Swarka and Naraka are the equivalents of the West's heaven and hell and are mentioned in the Puranas. The Swarka Lokas are the abode of the Devas and seem like welcome places to settle down after life, while the twenty-eight levels of torture cells in the Naraka are places to avoid. But while Christians and Muslims believe heaven and hell exist forever, Hindus regard them as temporary resting places for souls that never attained moksha.

Entry into Swarka or Naraka is decided by the Lord of death, Yama, and his karmic accountant, Chitragupta, who maintains the track record of each person during his or her lifetime. Stay at the Swarkas or Narakas is short. While those in Swarkas descend to earth as the karmic pious credits get used up, those in Narakas rise to the earth once due punishment has been meted out. They return to earth for another life and opportunity to liberate themselves from the cycle of birth and death. In Hinduism, the purpose of life is not to perpetually revolve around many levels of heavenly and hellish abodes, but to escape from the cycle of reincarnation. The permanent state Hindus aspire to is moksha, or merging with Brahman. It is seen as the soul's ultimate liberation from the cycle of life and death.

It may shock you to learn that although heaven and hell sound like after-death states, they are nothing but a figment of our imagination. So when scriptures talk about Swarkas and Narakas, what are they really saying? According to Hinduism, the human body exists at three levels: the gross physical, the subtle mental, and the causal. These roughly correspond to the body, mind, and the soul.[11] Obviously the physical body after death cannot travel to heaven or hell because all that is left of the body after cremation is the ashes. Similarly the causal body cannot travel, because the causal body is pure consciousness or Atman. The Scriptures repeatedly state that Atman is beyond the cycle of birth and death. So it seems the subtle mental body travels to heaven or hell after death and returns in a 'new' body. But the subtle body is really our mental recollections or unconscious tendencies and can make the journey only in the mind. This is what led Swami Vivekananda to interpret that heaven and hell are merely states of the mind.

In Hinduism, God does not create the world of heaven and hell, but we humans create a world of our own making after death. If our actions in our lifetime have earned us karmic credits, then our after-life experience will be heavenly as well. On the contrary, if our actions led us to earn karmic debits, our after-life experience will take us to hell. Thus the situation after life is entirely contrived by our own minds.

11 The soul in the Western world is sometimes attributed to the subtle mental body. Strictly speaking, there is no equivalent for the Atman.

32

All Paths Lead to God

Have you ever pondered this: If there's only one god for mankind, why are there so many religions in this world? Islam says the Koran is the true word of god and the only avenue to salvation. The Bible states Jesus is the only path to god. For Jews, Judaism is the way to God, while Mormons believe salvation can be obtained only through Joseph Smith and the Mormon Church.

In its own unique way, Hinduism says all paths lead to god. "Truth is one, but sages call it by different names," says the Vedas, the most sacred book of the Hindus. Hinduism allows not just one story of the world, but a slew of stories and philosophies. Each of these stories or beliefs leads to one supreme god. These stories are like fingers pointing to the moon. They should not to be mistaken for the moon but are pointers that help you understand the elusive nature of the universe.

When you ask people whether they believe in god, you are likely to get a variety of responses. Some will say, "Yes, I believe in a creator, for the universe is too complex to be just a coincidence," or "There got to be some order in this chaos." Others might say, "No, I don't see any evidence of god," or "Why this question? It's proven that Allah is the true god, since it says so in the Koran."

The basis for the Hindu belief that all paths lead to god is the recognition that each of us is special in our own unique way. Collectively we are the same predictable creatures, but as individuals there is diversity to our beliefs. Whether it is the quest for truth or adherence to a faith, the path that attracts us is the path that validates our beliefs and intuition. Like the spokes of a wheel, each path is unique and independent, yet each of them leads to the center of divine realization.

Like other religions of the world, Hinduism in itself offers many paths to reach god. Thus Shiva and Krishna and Sankhya and Vendanta are nothing but different means that validate your beliefs in pursuit of the truth. Yet Hinduism is changing and evolving. It demonstrates the religion's openness to new ideas and revelations. Hinduism was never founded on dogmas, for dogmas restrict the acceptance of new paths and resist the winds of change. It has always lent a welcome hand to the wisdom of sages—both old like Vyasa and Valmiki, and new, like Ramana Maharshi and Swami Vivekananda.

When you and I believe all religions lead to god, there is no need to wage wars or convert people to a fold. Hinduism has demonstrated this principle throughout its history. There was no missionary zeal to convert people to Hinduism, for it never prided itself as the only hope for salvation.

For thousands of years, India had been a home to devotees of every major religion. It was a safe haven for Jews, Christians, Buddhists, Zoroastrians, Sufis, and of course nonbelievers. There's no place in the world where religions coexisted and thrived in such close proximity as in India. The wisdom of its sages and the maturity of the tradition can be seen from its unparalleled tolerance to other religions. Among religions, Hinduism is the all-knowing mother.

So many gods, so many creeds,
So many paths that wind and wind,
While just the art of being kind
Is all the sad world needs
         – Ella Wheeler Wilcox (1855–1919)

We're definitely going to get Brooklyn christened, but we don't know into which religion.
         – David Beckham (1975–)

33

The Essence of Hinduism

So what exactly is the core of Hinduism? It is the story of a mysterious cosmic spirit that pervades, creates, and transcends all things. Hindus believe the universe is constantly changing, but beneath the evanescent nature of the world, there is a changeless, formless, all-powerful spirit called Brahman.

Brahman is God often personalized as Mother Goddess. It is the divine presence that creates and sustains all forms of existence. Much as Hindus believe Brahman pervades through the entire cosmos as consciousness, they also believe a part of Brahman exists in each human soul. The God in each person is called Atman.

It is believed the divine spirit often communicates with our inner consciousness. These messages are never heard because the human mind is preoccupied with worldly affairs. Just as the world is constantly changing, so is the mind as it goes through many impressions and thoughts. Moods shift and emotions fluctuate, even among those who are emotionally stable. Thoughts and sensations change with time, so do desires and opinions.

Hindus believe it is possible for the Atman in each soul to identify with Brahman at higher states of consciousness usually achieved through meditation.[12] As we probe deep into the consciousness of our

---

12 As discussed under yoga, meditation is one of the several paths to god.

own minds, we connect with the consciousness that underlies the entire cosmos. In profound meditation, when consciousness is acutely focused so that it's withdrawn from the body and mind, we enter a state in which the sense of ego as a separate identity disappears. In this supreme state of meditation, consciousness goes beyond time and change. It is in this state that the Atman of the soul merges with Brahman.

The aim of human life is to learn from inner experience Atman's identity with Brahman. It is when we purify our minds with spiritual practices that we begin to hear the messages from the divine spirit.

This, my friend, is the essence of Hinduism. When people say salvation in Hinduism is achieving the highest state of the mind, they are not off the mark. But this is just a simplification of its complex tradition. When you further explore the concepts of Maya, karma, dharma, samsara, and moksha, you've taken the whole of its vast traditions, but that's another story to tell.

The idea of cosmic consciousness has been explored in places far beyond the realm of Hindu mystics. It was accidentally discovered by a Canadian doctor named Richard Burke in 1876 and was explored by other Westerners like Jacob Boehme and Aldous Huxley.

34

Atman and Brahman – Self and Totality

Ever since the Upanishad famously said, "Tat Tvam Asi," meaning "you are that," Hinduism has been involved in an ongoing controversy over the distinction between Brahman and Atman. Although these two philosophical concepts of "self" and "totality" form the quintessence of Hinduism, their meaning is not fully agreed upon within the various traditions of the religion.

In the Chandogya Upanishad, a father tries to demystify the meaning of Atman to his son in everyday terms by asking him to cut a fruit from a banyan tree into half. "What do you see?" asks the father. "Tiny seeds," replies the son. The father then instructs the son to pick a single seed and cut into two. "What do you see now, son?" asks the father again. "Nothing!" answers the bewildered son. The father then explains to him that this nothing is the quintessence from which a vast banyan tree has grown. "That is the Atman, the essence of all things."

This analogy appears to suggest that Atman is different from Brahman. But the father has more to say.

Using an analogy of bees and their honey, the father goes on to explain that Atman is the self of the whole world. The bees prepare honey by gathering nectar from a variety of flowers. When the nectar from different flowers coalesces into a whole, you can no longer differentiate the individual nectar of each flower from its source. In the same way, when all living things merge into existence, they are not aware of being

101

a homogenous one. All creatures, without their knowledge, merge into the essence that constitutes the self of the universe. "You are that, you are that, son."

The more analogies are used, the more confusing the distinction becomes. The previous analogy would suggest that Atman and Braham, that is, the self in you and the universe, are identical. Thus, we are sparks from a single fire, and the fire is from our sparks. The question of whether Atman or Brahman represents a single principle or many is never conclusively answered in the Upanishads.

The Brhadaranyaka Upanishad uses another honey analogy to drive the point that Atman and Brahman are just parts of the cosmic oneness. "The earth is the honey of all beings, and all beings are the honey of this earth. The radiant and immortal person in the earth and, in the case of the body [Atman], the radiant and immortal person residing in the physical body—they are both one's self [Atman]. It is immortal; it is Brahman; it is the whole."

Thus the Upanishads seem to say, "Brahman is Atman. Atman is Brahman." This is perhaps the greatest timeless truth of Hinduism. It implies Atman and Brahman are parts of the same ultimate reality, which come together at the highest state of consciousness.

This message runs through the core of the Upanishads and indicates that all living beings, through self-discipline and spiritual discovery, can progressively merge with the cosmic oneness. The Hindu philosophy accepts that the mind and body are mortal, but the soul is immortal. As pure consciousness, Atman was never born because it existed all along. It therefore cannot die, but can only return to union with the Brahman. If Atman[13] is the consciousness of the individual, Brahman is absolute reality, or the source of everything.

Think the concepts of Atman and Brahman are mutually exclusive? In 1624, John Donne, the English poet and preacher, famously wrote, "No man is an island" in the passage that read, "No man is an island, entire of itself; every man is a piece of the continent, a part of the main. If a clod be washed away by the sea, Europe is the less... Any man's death diminishes me, because I am

---

13 Atman refers to the self of man, and it is not the ego. The ego is an idea and purely mental. The self constitutes the core of man's being and is different from the body, senses, and mind.

involved in mankind; and therefore never send to know for whom the bell tolls; it tolls for thee."

About 300 years later, Anne Morrow Lindbergh, American aviator and author, expressed the opposite idea, "I feel we are all islands—in a common sea."

How can both these statements be true even though they're mutually exclusive? Nobel prize winner Niels Bohr once said, "The opposite of a correct statement is a false statement. But the opposite of a profound truth may well be another profound truth."

35

Maya – The Power of Delusion

You and I live in a society that is so short on time and long on comfort that we have become too busy to notice we're busy. Trading our time for material possessions and personal freedom, we know our time on this planet is limited, yet we continue to live as if we are going to last an eternity.

Happiness is a point in the graceful arc traced by the pendulum of life. Sorrow is another. Everyone is searching for lasting happiness, yet we know it appears mysteriously during moments of joy followed by suffering in the journey we call life.

All these led Adi Shankara to believe our view of the world is simply a delusion, or, in his words, Maya. The limited knowledge gained from our senses and the mind fools us into thinking that this world is the only truth. Shades of truth, partial truths, twisting of the truth, and spin are blissfully accepted as truths and become the physical reality in which you and I live.

Maya is the veil that covers the truth and is formed when the Atman becomes trapped inside a physical body. Without a body, Atman cannot say "I." And without Atman, the body cannot say "I." But when the Atman and the body meet, a mysterious power of delusion is created in the form of "I-ness" and manifests among us as ego. Maya is the cloud that obscures the sun. It is the rope that is mistaken for a snake in twilight.

On seeing the rope, you jump out in fear because darkness has switched your mind into fright mode.

According to Shankara, the root cause of Maya is ignorance. To unveil the delusion of Maya, we have to free ourselves from our world of physical reality. Shankara contends that so long as Atman is bound to the body, Maya will continue to enchant the mind. The veil of Maya can be pierced only at the highest state of consciousness when the soul attains moksha and merges with Brahman.

For mere mortals like us, what are the implications? Are we forever destined to be slaves of Maya and therefore can do nothing much other than enjoy life to the fullest by retreating "to a coastal fishing village, where we could bask in the sun all day, sleep late in the night, play with the kids, take siesta at noon with wife Maria, and stroll through the village in the evening, sipping wine and playing guitar with amigos,"[14] right?

Not quite. For Shankara, Maya and moksha are like darkness and light. If one exists, the other cannot coexist. You can break away from the shackles of Maya by achieving Moksha. Moksha can be achieved by knowing the true identity of self through jnana (knowledge) yoga.

Among the philosophers of ancient India, Shankara was the foremost and is credited with founding Advaita Vedanta, which became one of six philosophical schools of Hinduism. Ahead of his times, Shankara attracted scathing criticism for his views, but most criticisms were leveled at his theory based on the misplaced notion that the world was a Maya. Shankara never suggested the world was an illusion. All he stated was the world appears to be a Maya because of ignorance. Over the years, several variations of his theory took hold, while Maya established itself as a dominant theme in Hinduism. For Shankara, jnana yoga was one of the key paths to eliminating ignorance and achieving moksha. It was even superior to bhakti yoga.

It should be remembered that Maya does not always mean delusion in Hinduism, underscoring the multi-traditional roots of Hinduism. In some philosophical system, it refers to the cosmic energy of the Supreme Being. Maya is also a popular name in Hinduism. In this context, Maya is considered a form of Lakshmi, particularly in Devi Mahatmyam, where

---

14 The part about having siesta with Maria was taken from Rob Parsons's book *The Heart of Success*

she is known as Mahamaya. In addition to these instances, Maya also makes a cameo appearance as a demonic character in the Hindu epic Ramayana.

> *This Indian doctrine declares human cognition of the entire manifold universe to be illusionary in character ... Man and his material environments were but finite dreams passing through the mind of the Infinite Dreamer. Consequently all that we know of the world is nothing more or less than a series of ideas held in our consciousness.*
>
> – Ralph Waldo Emerson (1803–1882)

36

Reincarnation

Shanti Devi pined to be home with her family, but when she spoke to her parents that she must return to her husband and son in Mathura, no one listened. Not many people pay attention to a little four-year old girl when she talks about her husband and son! Little Shanti pressed on and continued to talk about her previous life to everyone she knew. Out of curiosity, one of her teachers at school sent a letter to the address Shanti gave him. To his surprise, he received a reply from Shanti's previous husband, admitting his young wife had passed away some years ago, after giving birth to her son—exactly how Shanti had described.

And thus began in the 1930s one of the best documented and authenticated cases of reincarnation in modern history. This story soon captured the interest of people worldwide, including Mahatma Gandhi. A team of researchers, working under stringent conditions to ensure that Shanti couldn't have access to information from other sources, accompanied the little girl to Mathura, a little town about 150 kilometers south of New Delhi, India. She correctly described not only her former house but also her husband's cloth shop nearby. And she was able to lead them to her previous home on her own, where she met her son now older to her by a year.[15]

---

15 See the book *I have lived before: The True story of the reincarnation of Shanti Devi*, written by Swedish journalist Sture Lonnerstrand after spending several weeks interviewing Shanti Devi.

Luckily Shanti Devi lived in a country that routinely believes in reincarnations. The West has less than a passing interest in reincarnations. You are born one day, you have fun, and then you are gone. Talk about reincarnation to someone in the West, and you'll get the sort of look reserved for those who sighted a UFO, the wonderment and sense of disbelief as if you've gone out of your mind. With a worried face, they will come close to you, place a hand on your shoulder, and then in a faint whisper tell you: "Find a shrink!"

That's exactly the advice twenty-seven-year old Catherine received in 1980. Suffering from anxiety, panic attacks, and phobias, she went to Dr. Brian Weiss, a traditional but highly respected psychotherapist. Conservative in his approach, Dr. Weiss distrusted anything that could not be proven by traditional scientific methods. Initial therapies contributed very little to assist Catherine in overcoming her traumas, but after eighteen months of therapy, Dr. Weiss changed his approach and tried hypnosis, which, he wrote, was "an excellent tool to help a patient remember long-forgotten incidents....Under the instruction of a trained hypnotist, the patient's body relaxes, causing the memory to sharpen... eliciting memories of long-forgotten traumas that were disrupting their lives."

What unfolded at the subsequent sessions rattled Dr. Weiss out of his conventional thought and psychiatry. In a series of hypnotic trances, Catherine recalled past life memories and remembered living 86 times in physical state in different places on this earth both as male and female. She recalled distinctly the intimate details of each birth including her name, family, physical appearance, the landscape, and how she had died each time—stabbing, drowning, or illness. And in each lifetime she experienced a plethora of events "making progress... to fulfill all of the agreements and all of the karmic debts that are owed." For the first time, Dr. Weiss came face-to-face with the concept of reincarnation, which, as he says, "I thought only Hindus... practiced."

After Dr. Weiss published his findings,[16] he expected a skeptical world at large. Much to his surprise, he was taken seriously by many in the medical community. Psychiatrists have long observed many patients

---

16 See the book *Many Lives, Many Masters* by Dr Brian Weiss.

go back to something of a previous life during hypnosis which medical practitioners were always afraid to speak about.

History is littered with stories about reincarnation. I just picked two well-documented cases. Historically, the idea of reincarnation was not exclusive to Hinduism or Eastern religions. Belief in reincarnation (or gilgul) existed in Judaism until early in the 1800s, before it went underground. In Christianity the idea of reincarnation existed until the 6th century, when it was officially declared a heresy[17] at the Second Council of Constantinople.

Although disapproved by Western religions, the belief in reincarnation is popular among a few Westerners,[18] prominent among them being George Harrison of the Beatles fame, who believed that "life on earth is but a fleeting illusion edged between lives past and future beyond physical mortal reality." Speaking on reincarnation in 1968, he said: "You go on being reincarnated until you reach the actual Truth. Heaven and Hell are just a state of mind. We are all here to become Christ-like. The actual world is an illusion."

> *The living thing that goes on, always has been, always will be. I am not really George, but I happen to be in this body.*
> – George Harrison (1943–2001)

---

17 Christianity was becoming a state religion about that time and the Romans thought that people wouldn't behave without the fear of Judgment Day.
18 According to a 2008 Harris poll, 24 percent of Americans say they believe in reincarnation.

37

The True Self

The Chandogya Upanishad relates the tale of Indra and Virochana, the lords of the devas (gods) and asuras (demons) respectively, who set out to meet Prajapati,[19] the lord of the creatures, under the pretext of understanding the meaning of true self. With such enthusiastic, high-profile deities coming from afar, Prajapati was surprised but was more than happy to receive them as his students and impart his knowledge. After thirty years of teaching, Prajapati could no longer hold back his curiosity and demanded in no uncertain terms the real purpose of their scholarship.

"Lord, we both wish to understand the meaning of true self that would provide us immunity from illness and death and lead us to vanquish our enemies, conquer the world, and fulfill all our cherished dreams," replied his pupils.

Holding a large vessel containing water, Prajapati ordered each of his students to look into the vessel and describe what they see. "Lord, we see the whole of ourselves, even down to our hair and nails," replied Indra and Virochana in unison.

Prajapati then asked them to put on their finest clothes and look at themselves again in the water. Once again looking at their reflection,

---

19 As far as the early Vedas are concerned, the nature gods of Vedas were subordinated to Prajapati. Then in Upanishads, Prajapati was subordinated to Brahman, and the nature gods, including Sun, Agni, Vayu, Indra, and even Prajapati became servers of the highest.

"Lord, we see the self, exactly like ourselves, well adorned in our finest clothes," replied the lords of gods and demons.

And then said Prajapati, "The self is indeed seen in these images. That self is deathless and fearless, and that is the true self."

While Indra had his doubts, the demon king was completely convinced. Delighted at having found the ultimate insight into the self, Virochana triumphantly returned to the demons and soon formulated what became the guiding principle of the asuras. The body alone is to be served and materialistic pursuit will lead to the ultimate wisdom of the self.

It was only a matter of time for Indra to see through the falsity of the argument. "When the body is well-adorned, the self is well-adorned, but when the body becomes old or lame," thought Indra, "the self can become old and lame. When the body perishes, the self shall perish too." It wasn't too long before Indra returned to his teacher for further inquiry into understanding of the self.

Another thirty-two years passes quickly before Prajapati reveals a further insight: "He who wanders about rejoicing in dreams is indeed the self. That self is deathless and fearless, and that is the true self."

Once again Indra was quizzical. "True it is," he said to himself, "that this new self does not become blind if the body is blind, or lame or deformed when the body becomes lame or deformed, but even in dreams the self is conscious of many sufferings. Many have even died from the psychological effects of potent dreams. The self identified with the dreamer cannot be happy all the time."

So once more Indra returned to Prajapati and stayed with him for another thirty-two years, at the end of which said Prajapati, "When a man is in deep sleep, dreamless and in perfect peace, he realizes the self. That self is deathless and fearless, and that is the true self."

Content to his heart, Indra departed but not for too long, for he could sense the fallacy of this knowledge. "When one is asleep," he thought, "one does not know oneself, so how can he be conscious of any existence, let alone happiness."

A routine has been set. Every time Prajapati reveals a pearl of wisdom, Indra is confused and returns to his master. This time was no different but, unlike earlier times, Indra was much closer to the truth. It took another five years to learn from Prajapati the ultimate truth about self.

"The body," said Prajapati, "is mortal and forever in the clutches of death, but within it resides the immortal self. The embodied self is always subject to pleasure and pain, joy and sorrow, ageing and death. Only when the self is free from all the bodily bonds, you will find immortality and eternal bliss."

What Prajapati was teaching Indra over a hundred years was the distinction between the four states of consciousness and the accompanying perceptions of reality. In the waking state or the lowest form of consciousness, the self is attached to the material world through the mind and senses. It is filled with rational thoughts that are subject to the time and space constraints of the physical world. The next state of dreaming provides a higher level of perception, and the self is aligned to the body and mind but the senses are switched off. The dreaming self is no longer tied to the laws of logic or the constraints of time and space, and the mind starts playing games.

In the next state of dreamless sleep, the self is still connected to the body, but the senses along with the mind are cut off from the body. There exists no mind games in this state and hence it is considered blissful. The highest state, however, is the fourth state, known as turiya, in which the self is completely detached from the body, mind, and the senses. This is the pure consciousness and the nature of true self—immortal, blissful, and independent—which Hindus call Atman.

38

Brahman

It's the Vedic times. The famous sage Yajnavalkya, well known for his mastery of the Vedas, is being pummeled with questions at a debating contest by sage Gargi in the presence of the king and several scholars at the royal court.

"All this earth is woven, like warp and woof, in water. Upon what, then, are the waters woven and re-woven?" quizzes Gargi.

"In air, O Gargi!" answers Yajnavalkya.

"In what then is air woven, like warp and woof?"

"In the worlds of the sky, O Gargi," replies Yajnavalkya.

"In what then, are the worlds of the sky woven, like warp and woof?"

The incessant questioning goes on in this line until the entire cosmology is played out. Yajnavalkya, meanwhile, is a bit frustrated with this continuous stream of questions. Gargi, however, presses on relentlessly.

"In what then are the worlds of Prajapati woven, like warp and woof?"

"In the worlds of Brahman, O Gargi," replies Yajnavalkya.

"In what then, are the worlds of Brahman woven, like warp and woof?"

Inside Yajnavalkya was fuming and wanted to grab Gargi by the scruff of her neck and hurl her downward from the edge of a cliff, for it is not unusual for men of higher standing to become annoyed when pressed with profound questions that demand answers with black-and-white certainty. Yet Yajnavalkya, according to the Brihadaranyaka Upanishad, was never known to be discourteous to anyone. Instead Yajnavalkya responded thusly,

"O Gargi, do not ask too much lest thy head should fall off. Thou askest the Deity about which we are not to ask too much. Do not ask too much, O Gargi!"

The truth is Brahman cannot be described, for Brahman is that changeless, formless underlying reality that pervades, creates, and transcends everything, including our world and each of us. While the world is undergoing a ceaseless process of change, Brahman is changeless. If Brahman is the infinite ocean, we are ripples that form at a particular instance and die with the passage of time.

Brahman is God without attributes, limits, or characteristics, which Hindus call Nirguna Brahman. Anything that could be conceived or described cannot be Brahman, because that would limit by definition. Although Brahman cannot be known, it can be experienced at the highest state of consciousness. The scriptures state that the most one can say about Brahman is "sat-chid-ananda," meaning "existence-consciousness-bliss."

Yet there will be times when people like Gargi, peering the world through a weaving loom, will pester you relentlessly for a description of Brahman. Most people cannot worship something that is beyond description. And thus the concept of Saguna Brahman, or Brahman with attributes, was born to help people focus their mind and serve the lord.

It was precisely for this reason that Shiva and Vishnu and Lakshmi and Saraswati and another 330 million gods came into existence in Hinduism.

39

Darshanas

A Sanskrit word, darshan, refers to the act of seeing, particularly a god or a holy person. Darshanas, by extension, mean views, but they commonly refer to the six principle systems of Hinduism philosophy. Hinduism recognizes that my view and your view of life can be entirely different. The diversity in Hindu philosophy signifies that none of us are alike in our beliefs and convictions.

The darshanas, or the six Hindu philosophical schools, belong to the astika traditions, whereas Buddhism, Jainism, and Carvaka are nastika traditions that openly reject the teachings of the Vedas. Carvaka, an atheistic school of Indian philosophy, existed from about 600 BCE to 1400 CE. It was a hedonistic school of thought, advocating the nonexistence of the afterlife.

The six darshanas are as follows:

1. Sankhya – oldest and a dualist school of thought
2. Yoga – emphasis on meditation
3. Nyaya – based on logic
4. Vaisheshika – deals with the atomic nature of the universe
5. Mimamsa – an anti-ascetic and anti-mystic school
6. Vedanta – an anti-ritualistic but pro-mystic philosophy

If you think all these darshanas are alive and kicking, you are mistaken. Yoga and Vedanta, along with their subdivisions, are the leading philosophies of India. While both Vaisheshika and Mimamsa were rendered obsolete by the end of the 16th century, Nyaya survived a bit longer until about the 17th century. The oldest school, Sankhya, which does not accept the existence of God, lost its independence and merged with Yoga and Vedanta.

The Yoga philosophical system, expounded by sage Patanjali, is closely allied with the Sankhya school. It accepts the Sankhya psychology and metaphysics, but is more theistic than Sankhya. We will have more to say about these darshanas at a later time.

40

Ganesha

With an elephant head and the body of man, Ganesha at first appears ungainly to the eye, but among the Hindu gods, he is undoubtedly the most popular, and his popularity has spread into religions like Buddhism and Jainism. Images of Ganesha can be found not just in temples and home shrines, but in unusual places like automobiles, office desks, and even bedrooms. The son of Shiva and Parvati, Ganesha is depicted as having a potbellied body, large ears, and a trunk sampling a delicacy.

To be true, Ganesha is a lesser god and not in the same major league as gods in the Hindu trinity of Brahma, Vishnu and Shiva. As the son of Shiva, Ganesha is only a second-generation god and the leader of ganas (semi-divine followers of Shiva), but the popularity of Ganesha stems from his benevolence as the remover of obstacles and the granter of wishes. Buying a car, starting a company, writing a book, purchasing a home—in fact few auspicious moments in life are embarked upon without first seeking Ganesha's blessing. Known to have a delightful sense of humor (see Milk Miracle) and a sweet tooth, Ganesha is called Ganapathi or Vinayaka in South India.

Many stories abound about the origin of his elephant head. In one story, Parvati was feeling lonely, as Shiva had gone into retreat for meditation, and she decided to create a son from the scurf of her body. Ganesha was thus born to the world and initially enrolled his services as

Ganesha

a footman to his mother. When Shiva came home, the newly appointed guard did not recognize the visitor and refused entry. A furious Shiva ripped the head off his stubborn guard, not realizing the person was his own child. Parvati was filled with sorrow, but Shiva consoled her with the promise that he would replace the head with that of the first living creature he met. Along came by an elephant.

That was not the only time Ganesha got into trouble for diligently doing his duty. In another story, Parasurama, an avatar of Vishnu and a favorite disciple of Shiva, paid a visit to Shiva at his abode of Mount

Kailash. Once again, Ganesha was at the door and once again refused entry to the visitor, for he didn't want to disturb the sleeping Shiva. Soon a fight ensued. Ganesha picked up Parasurama with his long trunk, gave him a mighty twirl until he was dizzy, and threw him to the ground. When Parasurama came to his senses, he took his famous ax and flung it at his opponent. (The ax was given to him by none other than Shiva.) Ganesha recognized the ax, but, being an obedient son, he did not insult his father by resisting the weapon. And the ax broke his tusk, leaving him with only one tusk.

This explains the mystery of the missing tusk, but a different version, as is common in Hindu mythologies,[20] describes that Ganesha lost his tusk when he was asked to write down the epic Mahabharata by the author sage Vyasa while he dictated the story to Ganesha. Knowing the significance of the task, Ganesha realized the inadequacy of any ordinary writing tool and broke one of his own tusks to create a pen. For that reason, Ganesha is invoked as a patron of letters during writing sessions. Nowadays it is customary for writers to invoke Ganesha in their works as an epigraph.

In images of Ganesha you will find a rat near the foot as if it has accidentally wandered into the scene. Shiva rides a bull, Parvati, a lion, but the portly Ganesha moves around on a measly rat. Unfair and out of place, you may think, but Ganesha is an intelligent god and smart enough to know his limitations, as this story proves. Once Parvati asked her two sons, Ganesha and Kartikeya, to go around the world in a race. The brawny Kartikeya strutted off in his peacock knowing well that he would circle the globe faster, but on reaching home, he was stunned to learn that his brainy brother had beaten him to the punch. Ganesha had won without leaving the room. All Ganesha did was to circle around his mother and plead endearingly, "You are my world!" which melted Parvati's heart.

Most Hindus think of rats as pesky pests and carriers of diseases, but some devotees took their affection for Ganesha to a different level. In the late 19th century, when the British campaigned to exterminate rats, many Hindus in western India resisted the effort because of the animal's

---

20 Several stories of the same event are common in Hinduism. Often they have several interpretations and morals attached to them, underscoring the antiquity of the religion and its traditions.

association with Ganesha, thereby allowing bubonic plague to take its toll.

Hindus pay respect to their most popular god by enthusiastically celebrating the birthday of Ganesha nationwide, particularly in Mumbai, Maharashtra. Called Ganesha Chaturthi, the festival spans over ten days in which temples and homes are decorated with leaves and flowers. A large clay image of Ganesha is created for worship especially for this event. At the end of this festival, Ganesha is farewelled by carrying the clay image on a palanquin, bedecked with flowers, and then ceremoniously dipped into the ocean.

41

Chakras – The Energy Centers of the Body

Long lines were not unusual at the meat shop on the ground floor of Arya Bhavan, a dilapidated seven-story building. But next to the meat shop, hidden under the wooden stairs, stood the entrance to the magical elevator. I swear I had passed it a thousand times without noticing—until today.

Collapsible doors greet me at the elevator as I fumble with the buttons in the darkness. I press number two. The magical ride has begun.

A dimly lit shop comes into view at the next level. An elderly man stands solemnly at the counter. With curtains drawn tightly, there is no natural light inside. Occasionally a customer walks into the shop through a discreet entrance. There are no greetings or handshakes at the adult bookstore.

Faint sunlight greets me at the third level, where I see a group of people squabbling among themselves. Someone shouts, another one swears. The investment company has fleeced its customers. I quickly make my way back into the elevator.

As the brightly lit office of the Red Cross comes into display at the next level, the stench and the stealth of the previous levels seems to have gone. The elevator takes me next to a Vedanta school, followed by a meditation center, after which it wouldn't go any further. I was relieved. The darkness and the gloominess of the bottom floors have disappeared.

I am curious as to what awaits me at the last level.

Walking up the stairway, I am led into the open as I look around for a few minutes. There's nothing unusual, but then an astounding realization. With the azure blue skies above me and the warm earth decked with green trees beneath me, the view was magnificent, the panorama spectacular. I have reached the seventh floor or the pinnacle of the Chakras.

Arya Bhavan was my fantasy. The building is your body. The floors are the Chakras. And the elevator is the conduit through which energy flows upward. According to Hinduism, the human body contains seven Chakras or wheels, starting from the base of the spinal cord and extending to the top of the head. The Chakras are neither visible to the naked eye nor revealed during an autopsy, but they are centers of the body's energy system.

Hindus believe the Chakras interact with the body's ductless endocrine glands and lymphatic system by supplying good bio-energies and disposing of unwanted bio-energies. Chakras are not a recent discovery, for they have existed all along. In fact much of the information about the Chakras comes from the Upanishads.

The first Chakra, located at the base of the spine, represents the basic human need for survival, i.e., killing and eating. The meat shop at Arya Bhavan represents this level. Located near the genitals, the next Chakra represents procreation through which species propagate, as symbolized by the adult bookstore. The third Chakra represents our will to assert power and influence over others. The investment company at Arya Bhavan symbolizes our desire to acquire wealth and material gains.

While the first three Chakras characterize the basic animal instincts in humans, the next three represent the positive qualities of human beings. These higher Chakras represent the noble qualities that all religions espouse. The fourth Chakra, at the level of the heart, denotes compassion and altruism. When you open your heart, you elevate yourself from the level of an animal. Located at the level of throat, the fifth Chakra symbolizes spirituality, as represented by the Vedanta school. The sixth is the center of intuition and understanding. Through meditation, you learn to trust your inner guidance. The seventh Chakra, residing at the top of the head, represents cosmic consciousness. It corresponds to moksha or enlightenment. (Some Hindus believe that the magical elevator goes down from the base Chakra to another seven levels.)

According to Tantra Yoga (a variation of Raja Yoga), a mysterious power lies dormant in all human beings at the base of the spine corresponding to the first Chakra. Called Kundalini, the power is symbolically represented by a serpent coiled three and half times. When awakened by meditation, the Kundalini begins to move upward, activating the Chakras one by one, making the mind less physical and more spiritual. When it activates the seventh Chakra, spiritual energy merges with spiritual awareness. The mind then enters samadhi and the individual attains moksha.

Chakras are believed to be the nexus points of energy originating from Brahman, the ultimate reality in Hinduism. According to Tantra literature, Shakti (the feminine divine force) passes through the third eye on the forehead to lodge in the crown Chakra. Shakti then moves down from the topmost Chakra to the lowest Chakra, where it gets stored in the base Chakra.

Kundalini is the concrete or solid form of Shakti present in every human. It is believed that the Kundalini accumulates from one incarnation to the next and grants its possessor a great deal of power should it be unlocked. The purpose of Tantra Yoga is to unleash the Kundalini lying dormant in every person and elevate it through the Chakras until it merges with God when it reaches the Crown Chakra.

The Hindu Chakras

1. Muladhara - Base or Root Chakra (last bone in spinal cord -coccyx)
2. Swadhisthana - Sacral Chakra (ovaries/prostate)
3. Manipura - Solar Plexus Chakra (navel area)
4. Anahata - Heart Chakra (heart area)
5. Vishuddha - Throat Chakra (throat and neck area)
6. Ajna - Brow or Third Eye Chakra (pineal gland or third eye)
7. Sahasrara - Crown Chakra (top of the head; "soft spot" of a newborn)

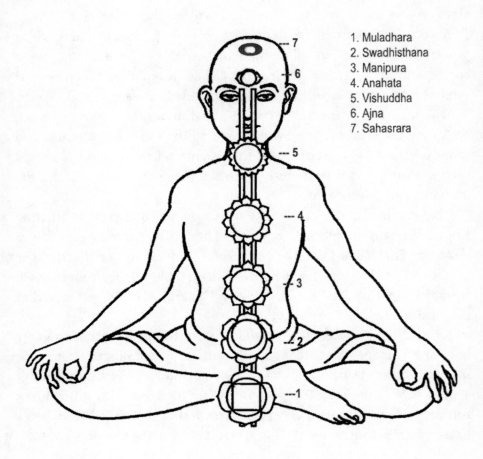

1. Muladhara
2. Swadhisthana
3. Manipura
4. Anahata
5. Vishuddha
6. Ajna
7. Sahasrara

The Hindu Chakras

42

Gayatri Mantra – Saluting the Sun

" Among the mantras, I am the gayatri" says Krishna in the Bhagavad Gita. Every day at dawn, just before the sun becomes fully visible, millions of Hindus recite a prayer called gayatri mantra as part of their rituals. Considered the most sacred mantra by practicing Hindus, and next only to Om, the gayatri, in Vedic hymnody, transliterates as follows:

Aum Bhur Bhuvah Swahah,
Tat Savitur Varenyam
Bhargo Devasya Dhimahi
Dhiyo Yo Naha Prachodayat.

Although the gayatri mantra can be chanted at any time of the day, scriptures recommend that you recite the gayatri as often as possible during sunrise until the sun's orb becomes fully visible in the horizon. Typically a Brahmin holds water in his right hand and, bringing it close to the nose, blows on the water first through the right and then through the left nostril. The gayatri is repeated three times before the water is poured out.

The gayatri mantra was first recorded in the Rig Veda, written in Sanskrit about three thousand years ago, and is attributed to Sage Vishwamitra. Since the gayatri was revealed to Vishwamitra by the

Sun god, the mantra invokes the solar spirit, whose body is the sun. Translated the mantra means:

> *We meditate upon the most radiant light of the Sun god,*
> *Who sustains the earth, the interspace, and the heavens*
> *May it awaken our intuitional consciousness.*

The most ancient method to establish communion with god was a solar yoga, and this tradition still lies at the heart of a Hindu yoga. The Hindus recognized that life was impossible on earth without the sun. So they celebrate and worship the solar spirit not only as the creator of life, but also as the principle that illuminates the mind.

The gayatri shares some magnificent similarities with many of the greatest prayers, such as the Fatiha, received by prophet Muhammad, and the Lord's Prayer, given to mankind by Jesus. In each of these great prayers, the opening lines are a humble recognition of a greater power that is beyond our understanding. The final lines then acknowledge the human gifts of understanding and awakening, which are continually bestowed upon mankind, even though few are aware of the gifts.

43

Mother Goddess

Sometimes life is wickedly cruel to the jewels of the community. Thirteen days after little Syama was born to this world and said hello with a cry, her mother bid goodbye and breathed her last. Her grandmother, who looked after her ever since, passed away before she even reached her teens. And soon after she was married at twenty, her father left the world. She had borne the brunt of setbacks early in her life what most people experience over a lifetime.

Yet life showed little mercy on her. The cruelest cut would come later, when her son died in an accident. As any mother will tell you, there is no sorrow greater than that of a parent who has lost a child. Life was asking Syama many questions that she had no answers for.

When faced with adversities in life, we, as humans, turn to something that will protect us from the vagaries of life. As young children, we look up to our parents as guardians to defend us in times of distress. When we grow older, we look to god to be our protector. It was only natural that religion became her sole solace in life, one that had the answers to her powerlessness and fear. Every day she would wake up early in the morning, put on her glasses, and diligently read the scriptures followed by pooja. Over the years, she visited many temples and learned from the gurus. Her passion for Hinduism soon attracted a long list of followers. One amongst them was I.

It was a medical wonder that Syama lived so long. As a child, she was inflicted with rheumatic heart disease that reduced her chances of survival. Despite heavy medical odds, she gave birth to three children, outlived all of her older brothers, and continued to lead a healthy life into her seventies without ever going under the knife. Just when everyone thought she might well go into her eighties or nineties, it came as a shock to learn the news of her death at the age of seventy-two.

The angst of losing my mother seems insignificant only when compared to the hardships she went through her life. Yet I am swamped with fond memories, as my voice chokes and a tear drops down my cheeks. The physical loss of someone who stayed close to your heart and enriched the meaning of your own life is excruciatingly painful—only those who experienced it would know. My rational side tells me time will heal all wounds, but I also know it will leave a few scars I will carry for the rest of my life. The spiritual essence of my mother will continue to live in the heart.

Out of love and respect, most people frame pictures of their mother in their living rooms. Some write books and dedicate them to their mother. Every year on the second Sunday in May, the world celebrates Mother's Day by showering gifts on living mothers. Hinduism has given birth to the loveliest and most sublime images of feminine divinity ever seen by the world. The worship of a god in the form of a mother is unique to the religion.

The idea of mother goddess or divine mother gained currency particularly after the composition of Devi Mahatmya (Glory of the Goddess) around 500-600 CE. Since creations evolve from the womb of the mother, the creative power of God is recognized as the female principle or the motherly aspect of nature. In the Hindu view, the universe is a manifestation of the creative power (shakti) of the ultimate reality Brahman.

The natural love between a mother and child is the best representation of god's unconditional love. When you go outdoors and connect with nature through her many manifestations as rivers, mountains, and the seas, you can feel the motherly affection of god. Living in seclusion for many years close to nature, American poet and naturalist Henry David Thoreau penned his experiences in his book *Walden*, which laid the foundation for modern environmentalism.

Thoreau's observations about nature came only in the nineteenth century what Hindus discovered several thousand years ago. From ancient times, rivers, mountains, hills, the sky, and in fact all of the earth, have been respected as the body of the goddess itself. In many parts of India, particularly in Bengal and Kerala, people worship mother goddess in many forms, such as Durga, Kali, Lakshmi, and Saraswati. The most notable among them was the worship of divine mother Kali by the famous Hindu sage Sri Ramakrishna Paramahamsa.

When you and I truly believe in mother goddess, there's no need for a party of greens, for no environmental program in the world can match the power of mother goddess.

> *Most of the luxuries and many of the so-called comforts of life are not only not indispensable, but positive hindrances to the elevation of mankind.*
>
> – Thoreau (1817–1862)

44

Yoga

Madonna swears by it, so do Meg Ryan and Ricky Martin. Yoga has become a popular fitness regimen of the modern era. Terms like "down dog," "flowering lotus," and "warrior pose" are familiar to most households these days, as yoga has become the standard way to exercise and reduce stress. From gymnastics to rugby, athletic programs now incorporate yoga for its systematic approach to stretching muscles, tendons, and joints. Yoga has become popular in major cities all over the world, especially so in Malaysia, where the Islamic authority issued a fatwa (religious edict) instructing the country's Muslims to stay away from yoga.

Let's be clear: fatwas are not legally binding. The Islamic council of Malaysia was merely pointing out the Hindu roots of the spiritual yoga, although the fitness yoga, the kind that is widely practiced these days, is devoid of any spiritual trappings. Meaning "yoke" or "unite" in Sanskrit, yoga has been in existence in India for thousands of years. Nobody knows its exact origins, but it is believed that about 200 BCE, a Hindu sage called Patanjali systematized and codified the ancient practices in a book called *Yoga Sutra*. Thousands of years of yoga tradition was thus condensed into 196 brief passages that defined the health practices and moral code of the yoga lifestyle. A yoga philosophical system was soon born under Patanjali, known as the father of yoga, and closely allied itself with the then existing Sankhya school.

After Yoga Sutra was published, yoga continued to evolve but only among Hindu ascetics living in isolation. It was Tirumalai Krishnamacharya, an influential Indian teacher and healer of the 20th century, who took yoga to the mainstream by teaching breath control when performing a continuous series of poses. Building on his work, three of Krishnamacharya's students developed their own yoga styles that define contemporary yoga practices. Pattabhi Jois refined the existing Ashtanga yoga into his own brand called Ashtanga Vinyasa yoga. B. K. S. Iyengar developed the gentler Iyengar style, where people performed yoga using props like blocks and straps. T. K.V. Desikachar, Krishnamacharya's son, introduced Viniyoga, a more versatile form of yoga with emphasis on postures. With its spiritual roots fading into oblivion, yoga thus morphed into many forms. Another popular yoga known as Bikram yoga or hot yoga and started by Bikram Choudhury is practiced in a room heated to 41degrees Celcius.

Yoga (Padmasana)

For the ancient Hindus, yoga was more than just a fitness routine. It was a spiritual routine, a means of uniting the individual with the Brahman or the individual consciousness with cosmic consciousness. Traditionally Hinduism offered four yogas or paths to enlightenment: Raja (meditation), Jnana (wisdom), Karma (service), and Bhakti (devotion). Each of these paths offers a series of steps to separate the ego from the real self (Atman), thereby achieving moksha. Thus yoga is nothing but the sifting of the non-self from the self, the unreal from the real. The four different paths underscore the fact that each of us is unique in our own way and may prefer one path over another.

Raja means "king" and Raja yoga is the royal road to spirituality. This is Pantanjali's classical yoga and is based on the premise that spiritual ignorance is the cause of suffering. There are eight aspects to Raja yoga, so sometimes this yoga is referred to Ashtanga (eight-limbed) yoga, although Patanjali himself preferred to call it "Kriya Yoga." The eight limbs are like props that assist in the progressive shift from the egoic identity. Although Raja yoga is the quintessential yoga, many variations of it have spawned over the years, including Laya yoga, Tantra yoga, and the ubiquitous Hatha yoga, the most popular yoga in the West.

Jnana yoga is the path to wisdom. Such wisdom is, however, not attained through knowledge as commonly understood. It is the rational inquiry into the self or the ability to discriminate between the real and unreal. Jnana yoga is the path of the Vendanta schools. Adi Shakara of the Advaita philosophy gave prime importance to Jnana yoga over other yogas. Others like Ramanuja considered wisdom only as a condition of devotion.

Bhakti yoga is the path of devotion. While it remains the predominant path toward spiritual fulfillment in Hinduism, Bhakti yoga is also the sole path adopted by major world religions, including Christianity, Islam, and Judaism, in serving god. In Bhakti yoga, devotees choose a deity and become committed,[21] observing selfless devotion to the deity in accomplishing their spiritual goals. Devotees engage in various activities like singing bhajans (devotional songs), offering flowers, and performing pooja (rituals). In the highest form of Bhakti yoga, devotees

---

21 According to American tennis player, Martina Navratilova: "The difference between involvement and commitment is like ham and eggs. The chicken is involved; the pig is committed."

go for complete surrender. Some of the great exponents of Bhakti yoga include Chaitanya and Meera Devi toward Lord Krishna, Tulsi Das toward Lord Rama, and in modern times Ramakrishna Paramahamsa toward goddess Kali.

Karma yoga is the path of right action. It teaches that work performed in the spirit of service and the welfare of mankind leads to moksha. Good actions bring one closer to the spiritual goal while bad actions take one farther away. An important aspect in the practice of Karma yoga is the total disinterest in what Lord Krishna calls the fruits of one's actions. Ordinarily, our actions are governed by so-called ulterior motives. In karma yoga, the emphasis is doing the right service in accordance with the social and spiritual wisdom of the day without attachment.

CONTROVERSIES

45

Idol Worship

Every Hindu temple and shrine is home to a vast number of deities in the form of pictures or statues to which Hindus pray by singing hymns or chanting mantras. Worship of gods through idols is a central theme of Hinduism. Attached to idols like a mother to child, Hindus are aware that the idol is not god but a symbol of god. But what they are not aware of is the longstanding notion in Western religions that says idolatry is evil. So ancient and deep-rooted is this misplaced belief that every major religion has succumbed to it.

Excuse me, why is idol worship so bad as it is generally believed to be?

History reveals that the belief perhaps started in the Jewish lore, where Abraham, the patriarch of Judaism, took a hammer and smashed the idols of his father, an idol merchant. At the time of Abraham, image worship was common among the pagans living in those regions. Soon the Jewish people abandoned paganism and accepted monotheism. However, it was through Judaism's offshoots of Christianity and Islam that much of the world came to reject paganism and polytheism and to adopt the concept of one god.

If you think about it, idols are nothing but symbols that provide a visual representation of ideas. As humans, we need symbols to visualize ideas and concepts that exist only in our mind. The national flag symbolizes the spirit of a nation. The Christian cross and the Jewish menorah are unique symbols representing Christianity and Judaism. A miniature model of a high-rise, an idol of a deity, or a picture of a family are merely expressions of human ideas and beliefs. While hoisting the flag or singing the national anthem is patriotic, why is worshiping the image of god not spiritual but evil?

The line of reasoning was that even though idols are representations of god, worship of idols can lead to the danger of becoming attached to the idols themselves. Soon the idols change themselves into self-contained powers in their own right. For the devoted, destruction of an idol becomes an attack on the religion, just as for a patriot burning a flag is an assault on the nation.

Among the Western religions, Judaism strictly forbids idol worship. Several places in the Hebrew Bible reinforce the idea that God has no shape or form and therefore no idol can ever capture God's essence. The contemporary Christian view of idolatry is largely inherited from Judaism, but it is more permissive, defining idolatry as the erroneous worship of an idea or object in place of worshiping the Holy Trinity. Images of Jesus are not explicitly forbidden. While Protestants believe in god's omnipotence and suspect idolatry as an object for manipulating god, Catholics generally approve the use of images in religious life, such as honoring the cross and deceased saints.

Muslims are fierce opponents of idol worship. Anti-idolatry sentiments are expressed more vehemently in the Koran than in any other scripture. Muslims were the first iconoclasts (literally, icon-smashers) and Indian history is replete with stories of Muslim rulers desecrating Hindu temples and vandalizing idols. Not too long ago, the colossal images of Buddha in the Bamiyan province of Afghanistan were razed to the ground by the Taliban in the name of abolishing idol worship. Many schools of Islam view the Christian belief in the Holy Trinity itself as idolatrous.

Contrary to popular belief, Hinduism neither prescribes nor proscribes the worship of images. Some Hindu sects, like the Arya Samaj and Brahma Samaj, do not believe in using idols as a way to focus on God. Most Hindus, however, worship god through idols. God is omniscient and idols represent different aspects of the divinity that appeal to devotees. Many Hindus claim in earnest that their idol is only a representation of the God, yet the Hindu tradition of giving absolute sanctity to temples and offering food to idols seem to indicate that the idols themselves are the deities.

Interestingly, although most Western religions forbid idol worship, idols depicting their founder or religious practices are acceptable. In short, no true definition of idol worship exists, with each religion holding its own interpretation of what constitutes an idol. The distinctions are blurry and often give rise to such absurdities as, "Should Christians have Christmas trees?" alluding to the popular belief that Christmas trees have pagan origins.

Yet no compelling grounds exist to say idol worship is evil. On the contrary, much killings and plunder around the world happened in the name of eliminating idol worship. Historians note that the spread of Christianity and Islam was accompanied by a good measure of killing pagans and destroying their places of worship. It appears the entire anti-idolatry plank of Western religions is just an ideological justification for the genocide of pantheistic pagan cultures.

The freedom to choose religion and the right to practice it is enshrined in the constitution of major nations. So long as these are legitimate means to reach god, no one has the right to deny them. Thus worshipping a Balaji in Tirupati, a Jagannath in Puri, a Nataraja in Chidambaram, a Krishna in Udupi, a Meenakshi in Madurai, a Varadaraja in Kanchi, and a Guruvayoor Appan in Kerala will always be some of the intimate ways Hindus strive to connect with god.

That idol worship is evil is just a lousy dogma.

46

Silence of the Buddha

There are certain individuals who shout for answers even for the most profound of questions. Monk Malunkyaputta was one of them, for he had doubts about Buddha's knowledge on philosophy. One day Malunkyaputta decided to find out the truth for himself. Addressing Buddha, he spoke thusly:

"Sakyamuni, I can no longer be satisfied with your silence to those questions of life that continue to astound me from dawn to dusk and dusk to dawn. If you shall agree to satisfy my curiosity, I promise I shall become a loyal follower for the rest of my life. However, if you choose to maintain your silence, I shall renounce the sangha and abandon the faith this very moment." Pausing to gather his breath, Malunkyaputta continued, "Now tell me the answers to these questions of life. Is this world eternal? Does the world extend to infinity? What's the difference between the body and soul? What happens to your body and soul after death? And finally will you Sakyamuni exist after death?"

On hearing these questions, Buddha felt that he could no longer continue his silence. So he spoke. "Malunkyaputta, you are like someone shot with a poisoned arrow, but refusing to pull out the arrow until you know who shot you and the motive behind it. Such a man will die before getting the answers. I teach only those things that are necessary. Things that are not helpful, I do not teach. Whether the universe is finite or infinite, temporal or eternal is best left to speculation, but there is one truth you must accept, and that is the presence of suffering."

Although Malunkyaputta did not press further and continued with the sangha, many thought Buddha was vague and evasive in answering the metaphysical. Although Buddha finally made his point, it answered a question no one was asking. Some thought he was not well-versed in philosophical matters. Others acknowledged Buddha was less interested in questions about the ultimate reality but more keen on the down-to-earth business of achieving nirvana, or escape from suffering.

Theory for its own sake was denounced by the Buddha. But theory in pursuit of enlightenment was encouraged, for behind the deceptively concise Four Noble Truths lies answers to questions on the nature of reality. In the so-called ti-lak-karma, the three general characteristics of existence are explained. First, nothing in this world is permanent. Like the flow of water in a stream, everything is constantly changing. Second, existence is characterized by suffering. Desire is the root of all suffering. The suffering is not because of the fleeting nature of things, but due to a lack of true understanding of reality. Third, the Hindu Atman or self does not exist and is an illusion created by a combination of mental and physical activities.

The Buddhist characterization of the self as an illusion was quite a radical line. It raised an important question: If there is no self, then how does rebirth take place?

The Buddhist scriptures explain this through the chain of causation. It means everything is caused or conditioned by everything else. Things are interconnected in such a way that you cannot separate the cause from effect. The self is the result of a chance happening when the right elements merge together within a period of time. Upon death, the consciousness, or the sense of self, of a person becomes one of the contributing causes for a new group of elements to form another self. The consciousness in this new person is neither identical nor different from the previous one. As long as ignorance exists, the self will perpetuate endlessly. The only means of escape from this relentless cycle is by overcoming ignorance through enlightenment.

For the monks in the sangha, the Buddhist thinking was intriguing if not mind-boggling. As Buddha said in the past, some things are best explained by silence rather than by shouting.

Of the great religions of history I prefer Buddhism, especially in its earliest forms because it has had the smallest element of persecution.

– Bertrand Russell (1872–1970)

47

Hinduism Vs. Buddhism

> *If you love the sacred and despise the ordinary, you are still bobbing in the ocean of delusion.*
>
> – Lin-Chi

My friend Premadasa is normally a boring, slumbering Koala during conversation. Mention religion and he wakes up from his sleep and turns into a vicious Sri Lankan sloth bear that hasn't eaten for months.

Today was one of those days. And I have just blurted out something about Buddha. The response was swift.

"Lord Buddha can never be an avatar of Vishnu. You see, both Hinduism and Buddhism are major, established religions of the world. In their long history, each influenced the other and shared a close relationship. Both originated in India, and of course, Hinduism predates Buddhism by at least a millennium or two. You got to remember that Buddhism evolved as a natural reaction to certain practices of Hinduism. So Buddha coming to this world as a Hindu avatar doesn't make sense."

It was my turn to respond. "I know you Buddhists don't subscribe to the idea of an avatar. It is a true but little-known fact that Buddha was born as a Hindu, lived as a Hindu, and died as a Hindu."

I was met with a long silence, for like a contemplative observer, Premadasa was lost in thought. But when he started talking, there was no stopping.

"Indeed Buddha was born as a Hindu, but you have to accept the striking differences between the religions. In principle, Hinduism is about the cosmos, whereas Buddhism is about the mind. Buddhism does not accept the Vedic theory on which Hinduism is based, instead it relies solely on the teachings of the Buddha. Even the concept of dharma is different. The Hindu dharma refers to right conduct based on religious and moral rights of an individual and depends on caste. Thus the dharma of a Brahmin is different from that of the Kshatriya because each caste has its own body of dharma. The Buddhist dharma, on the other hand, is much simpler and refers to religious truth; that is, Buddha's teaching as the highest truth."

Sure enough Premadasa was speaking the truth, but I wasn't prepared to quit.

"For you Buddhists, when it comes to metaphysics, everything is an illusion, isn't it? You reject the existence of a God, one who stands distinct and separate from humankind. You do not believe in the existence of Atman, or individual soul. You also do not believe in the ultimate reality or Brahman for that matter. Face it mate, you are a nontheistic religion. Aren't you?"

I could see Premadasa's eyes brighten up like a sloth bear that has just spotted a termite mound. Suddenly his lips turned into a vacuum-cleaner nozzle about to go deep into the mound and hungrily suck it clean.

"No, we don't believe in gods. In Theravada, the only god is the Buddha, and by following his teachings you can attain nirvana. Our concept of liberation is different from yours. Hindus refer to the liberation of soul as moksha, whereas we call it nirvana. In Hindu tradition, moksha is the reuniting of the Atman with Brahman. An Atman or soul can attain moksha only at the highest level of the caste system. To ascend to the highest level, a Hindu should perform his dharma and accumulate good karma. The caste at birth determines the social standing. It determines his profession, education, religious duties, and responsibilities. As can be evidenced throughout history, the caste system stood in the way of individual freedom and social progress. People of lower castes were entrenched at the lower level of the society without any hope for social advancement. Buddhism rejects the caste structure prevalent in Hinduism. In Buddhism, anyone could achieve nirvana and escape samsara by following Buddha's teachings. Surely you have to go through cycles of reincarnation to achieve nirvana, but there is no social order limiting your advancement in society."

My friend Premadasa was firmly in charge of our exchanges. Like a runner in the lead at the end of a marathon, he was about to cruise the last mile with no one behind him.

"To achieve enlightenment, the ideal approach in Hinduism is through extreme asceticism, which involves renunciation of worldly pleasures. Buddhism focuses on a middle way between extreme asceticism and extreme worldliness. Hinduism teems with deities. You Hindus worship god in the form of idols. We Theravadas, the original Buddhist followers, do not worship images of Buddha nor believe in bodhisattvas. Mahayanas, on the other hand consider Buddha as the supreme soul, akin to the Brahman of Hinduism, and practice idol worship."

And then came the finish.

"As you can see, Buddhism can be considered a reform movement, particularly aimed at eliminating practices like the caste disparity, idol worship, and extreme asceticism."

Premadasa has truly won this race, for I have been beaten hook, line, and sinker. Deep inside, I was glad this was over. But it got me thinking all night long. Something was wrong. How did Hinduism manage to hang around for so long without being wiped out from the face of the earth?

It took me many days and weeks to realize that, despite many weaknesses, Hinduism, the oldest religion in the world, has some incredible strengths. By abolishing the caste system in 1949, Hinduism proved it could rapidly eliminate certain time-honored traditions of the society. Its greatest strength was undoubtedly the ability to change through times and embrace new ideas. A shining example has been the acceptance of Buddhism. The Indian constitution, widely regarded as the longest ever written of any country, considers Hinduism a general religion that includes Buddhism and others like Sikhism and Jainism.

The ability to reform itself and evolve made Hinduism resilient through the times. Unlike other religions, Hinduism had long accepted that many paths lead to God. Throughout its history, Hinduism has accommodated both believers and nonbelievers, iconoclasts and idol-worshipers, liberals and conservatives. Today Buddhism[22] is the fourth largest religion in the world, with about 460 million followers. But more than one billion around the world call themselves Hindus.

In the final analysis:
1,000 million Hindus + 460 million Buddhists = 1,460 million Hindus

Surely including Buddhists under the category of Hinduism will incur the wrath of my friend Premadasa, but that's counting Indian constitution-style ☺.

> *To my mind Buddhism has always seemed to be not a new religion, but a natural development of the Indian mind in its various manifestations.*
>
> – Max Müller (1823–1900)

Estimated World Population (2011)

Religion	Size
Roman Catholics	1.2 billion
Muslims	1.6 billion
Hindus	**1.0 billion**
Nonbelievers	1.1 billion
Protestants	420 million

---

22 Buddhists spread from India throughout the East—Tibet, Southeast Asia, Korea, China, and Japan, where it merged with native traditions and changed form. Buddhism died out in India and established firmly on the island of Sri Lanka

Buddhists	460 million
Chinese folk religionists	450 million
Jews	14 million
Sikhs	24 million
Others	752 million
Total	**7.02 billion**

48

The Manly Englishman and the Effeminate Indian

Taking a page out of Darwin's theory of evolution, the German Indologist Max Müller invented his own theory of the evolution of religion in which he postulated that religions of the world are at various stages of development and had progressed linearly from a basic stage to the advanced. Seen in this light, Hinduism was in the primitive or infantile state of development, whereas Christianity had reached an advanced stage with a high degree of ethical and moral perfection. Some missionaries with evangelical leaning were skeptical of this theory, but Max Müller saw nothing unusual. That he happened to be a Christian missionary of an advanced religion was, well, just coincidence.

It was in this backdrop that British civil servants and missionaries arrived in colonial India and had their first glimpse of Hindu traditions. Hinduism appeared to be paganistic, primitive, and superstitious, and Hindu gods the embodiments of vice, lacking in moral virtues. The British believed that Hindus who engaged in idolatry imbibed the immoral qualities of their deities. The Rev. William Ward, the outspoken Baptist missionary, described the Hindus as "effeminate, deceitful, lazy, and ignorant." According to him, their feeble bodies were as a result of little exercise and excessive bookishness.

The colonial British stereotyped Indian men as soft, girly marshmallows, while females were fat globes concealed in saris. The quintessential symbol of Hindu effeminacy was the Bengali Babu or the typical government clerk. In a British account, Lord Macaulay states, "Whatever the Bengali does he does languidly…He shirks from bodily exertion; and scarcely ever enlists as a soldier. We doubt whether there be a hundred genuine Bengali in the whole army of the East India company."

The missionary concept of Hinduism as an effeminate religion formed the basis of the colonial portrayal of India as an effeminate nation lacking any sense of order, progress, or rationality. In British eyes, these effeminate souls required the straightforwardness of Christian honesty and the manliness of British men to restore order and stability. In short, only the manly British men, and not the effeminate Indian men, could be trusted to protect India and Indian women.

It seems dimwittedness was on the march in colonial India. Sir Winston Churchill wasn't exactly the epitome of English manliness. Although outwardly the British were seen projecting Indians as sissies and lazy, behind closed doors they were diligently assessing the risks possessed by various sects within India. Ethnic groups like the Sikhs, Pathans, Rajputs, and Nairs were classified as martial races, a term originally used by the English, who observed that certain ethnic groups were inherently more martially inclined than others. (The Scottish Highlanders, for instance, were more powerful in battle than others in Britain.) The famous martial art of the Nair community of Kerala called Kalari Payattu, believed to be the mother of all martial arts and from which Kung-fu evolved, was summarily banned by the British during their reign.

By the mid-20th century, the macho Englishmen received a rude shock when a thin, half-naked man brought the might of the British empire under his knees. The British used guns and cannons and mortars to subdue Gandhi and his resistance movement, but there's nothing much a manly Englishman can do when the opponent is not fighting. India was the first country in all of Asia and Africa to throw off the British colonial yoke in 1947. Independence in Afro-Asia followed only after India succeeded.

Although the typical Bengali Babu might look like Lord Ganesha reincarnated, historically Bengalis are known for their sharp intellect and revolutionary heritage. With such luminaries as Ravi Shankar, Ramakrishna Paramahamsa, Rabindranath Tagore and Vivekananda, the land of Bengal tigers had always been the cultural capital of India. During colonial times, nationalism first emerged in Bengal in the cultural and religious fields, particularly through the works of Bankim Chandra Chattopadhyay. Swami Vivekananda, another Bengali, saw nationalism through the prism of Hinduism. The metaphor of Bengal as the Mother Goddess, conceived by Bakim Chandra, was taken up by radical groups involving Bipin Chandra Pal and Aurobindo Ghose. If you thought Subash Chandra Bose, Raja Ram Mohan Roy and Sarojini Naidu were Babus languishing on a can of rasgullas, think again. Bengal was also the birthplace of the militant group called Naxalite, which today is categorized the most violent terrorist group by the government of India.

Unlike their male counterparts, not all Englishwomen regarded Indians as sissy and effeminate. Edwina Mountbatten found in Nehru what she couldn't find in a manly Englishman. If the Bengali Babu was the quintessential milksop, then Bhagwan Shree Rajneesh, with his prominent forehead and piercing eyes, was his polar opposite. Rajneesh has been called everything else except a sissy.

The population of India is surging, but Britain, like most Western countries, is struggling with a negative birth rate. Colonial men were long used to wielding guns, but it appears only the effeminate Indian men were carrying the loaded variety. It is said the only time the Englishmen truly fire is while rendering the 21-gun salute ☺.

49

Man Created God?

Among the poets to grace the land of Bharata,[23] one of my favorites was a little-known southerner called Vayalar. Having composed a litany of poetic pearls, Vayalar never became a household name in India because the entire poetry was composed in Malayalam, the language of Kerala.

One day Vayalar wrote these controversial lines:

Man created religions
Religions invented gods

And then mankind and religions and gods came together
And agreed to share the earth and the minds of people
.....

First a Hindu, then a Muslim, and later a Christian
Soon you became someone no one knows
For the whole world has degenerated into a mental asylum

...

...

---

23 Bharata is another name for India. The name comes from the Hindu epic Ramayana

What happened to the avatars of God
That come to this world once every 1000 yugas and rescue mankind
For when man dies in the streets, religions merely laugh

Obscure poetry at best, these lines caught the attention of a movie producer, who saw meaning and melody and used them as lyrics for a song. The rest is history. The movie was average, but the song, rendered in the golden voice of Jesudas, turned out to be utterly seductive among the people of Kerala, comprising Hindus, Christians, and Muslims. (We'll meet Jesudas again.) The song went on to become one of the greatest film hits ever. Vayalar Rama Varma won a national award for his composition. Jesudas won a national award for the best playback singer. For a song composed in a language spoken by less than 10 percent of the Indian population, the success was incredible.

How could a song that says gods were the creation of people become so popular in a conservative country dominated by Hindus? Vayalar wrote this song in the 1970s. In those days, poets simply blurted out the truth. Political correctness did not cloud their thinking. Religious fanatics haven't taken over the world. Time hasn't dawned upon a well-known Christian preacher to appear on TV and make an absurd statement like, "Help us carry the light to a nation in darkness."

Vayalar was a Kerala[24] communist. In his native state, a communist is tantamount to an atheist. Yet Vayalar was a staunch Hindu. The song was aimed at national unity among multiethnic Indians but was pitched at the epicenter of Hinduism.

Hinduism did not retaliate, for Vayalar was neither excommunicated nor regarded as an outcast. As a Hindu, you can be an ardent devotee or a caustic atheist. It was Mahatma Gandhi who famously declared that you could be a Hindu without believing in any god. In fact some of the older philosophical schools, such as Sankhya, do not even postulate the

---

24 The birthplace of Adi Shankara, Kerala is at least thirty years ahead of other Indian states in thinking and way of life. It is the only state in India where the impoverished look healthy and the beggars are hundred percent literate. Unlike the rest of India, Keraleans think movie superstars are superheroes only in celluloid and do not necessarily make great chief ministers. Swami Achuthananda pins it down to one thing: coconuts. Keraleans use coconut oil for cooking and as hair oil. While the coconut-rich food nourishes the body, the hair oil energies the brain.

152

existence of god. It was gratifying to see the award committee uphold the tradition of the nation and award the highest honor to the creator of the song.

Lest you thought so, Vayalar was not the first to deny the existence of gods. The famous creation hymn[25] known as Nasadiya from the Vedas proclaim (see the fourth stanza):

In the beginning there was neither non-existence nor existence then;
There was neither the realm of space nor the sky which is beyond.
What stirred? In whose protection?
Was there water, bottomlessly deep?

There was neither death nor immortality then.
There was no distinguishing sign of night nor of day.
That one breathed, windless, but its own impulse.
Other than that there was nothing beyond.
In the beginning was love,

Which was the primal germ of the mind.
The seers searching in their hearts with wisdom
Discovered the connection between existence and non-existence ...

The gods were later than this world's creation –
Therefore who knows from whence it came?
That out of which creation came,
Whether it held it together or did not,
He who see it in the highest heaven,
He only knows – or perhaps even He does not know.

---

25 This translation is from Wendy Doniger.

Everyone has faith in God though everyone does not know it. For everyone has faith in himself and that multiplied to the nth degree is God. The sum total of all that lives is God. We may not be God, but we are of God, even as a little drop of water is of the ocean.
– Mahatma Gandhi (1869–1948)

50

Sin and Paapa

Regardless of whether you've been a good, honest citizen of higher standing, the gospel truth is you are a sinner. It's not just you, we are all sinners in God's eyes. As a descendant of Adam, you and I have inherited the "original sin," which was committed by Adam and Eve when they ate the forbidden fruit in the Garden of Eden. "All have sinned, and come short of the glory of God," says the Bible (Romans 3:23).

The original sin, according to Christian theology, is shared by everyone and can be removed only by faith in Jesus. Compared to original sin, actual sin (the sin created in the present life) can be removed, but the way in which it is eliminated has created the great division between Catholics and Protestants. The Protestants say faith in Jesus is the only way to remove that sin too, whereas Catholics resort to a complex system of confessions and penance.

The Western concept of sin does not exist in Hinduism. Man is born not as a sinner, rather as a potential divine being. The Sanskrit word "paapa" is often translated as sin, but there is a key difference. Sin is a crime against the will of God, while paapa is a violation of moral order or dharma. According to Hinduism, man commits paapa because of ignorance of his true self. Paapa includes all kinds of wrongdoing, from the simplest infraction to the most heinous crimes and creates a karmic burden. To offset paapa, Hindus carry out penances that settle the karmic debt. Penances range from chanting mantras, prostrating at the feet of a deity, fasting for days, or performing austerities.

Although paapa can be resolved by undertaking penances, the key to avoiding paapa is through enlightenment. Just as it does not subscribe to the idea of sin, Hinduism does not believe in Christian concepts like salvation[26] or hell. When there is no sin, no salvation is needed, only enlightenment. And when there is no sin, there is no eternal hell. For Hindus, hell and heaven are only states of the mind.

Yet many Hindu writers trained in Christian schools mistakenly assume paapa as Western sin. While sin is linked to hell, paapa affects the karmic debit of the present life. Karma accrued from past lives can be eliminated not through penances but by meditation or by seeking the extraordinary grace of God through devotion.

---

26 Moksha is sometimes referred to as salvation although the two are different.

156

51

The Hindutva Movement

Like most people, I have my pet peeves, but unlike many of you, I am aware of them and have learned to keep my brand of peeves to myself. One of my pet peeves is against the Hindutvas, but I must confess that it has nothing to do with their ideology to preserve Hindu heritage. On the contrary, I feel a nationalistic movement that lends a united voice for India, especially when it comes to debunking myths like the Aryan Invasion Theory, can be quite powerful.

So what is Hindutva? Although the notion of Hindutva or "Hindu-ness" has been around since the days India was invaded by foreigners, particularly the Islamic invasions in the 8th century CE, most people nowadays equate Hindutva to Hindu militancy dressed up as Hindu nationalism. The word Hindutva was coined by Veer Savarkar, a great theoretician of the nationalistic movement called Hindu Mahasabha, in his 1923 pamphlet entitled *Hindutva: Who is a Hindu?* The Hindu Mahasabha was founded with a mission to give Hindus a political vote. It proclaimed Hindustan as the land of the Hindus, demanding the right to govern themselves according to Hindu laws. During British rule, Veer Savarkar exhorted Hindus to rise up to the British and drive them out of India. Like other Hindu political organizations, the Hindu Mahasabha contained a strong anti-Muslim sentiment that increased with the creation of Pakistan. After independence, he urged the Hindus to make India a Hindu country by overthrowing Nehru's secular government and militarizing Hinduism. His firebrand speeches ensured long spells of imprisonment under the British and house arrest under the Congress party.

Another Hindu militant movement in the 1900s was the Rashtriya Swayemsevak Sangh or RSS. It was founded by Keshav Hedgewar, a medical doctor who practiced nationalism instead of medicine after witnessing the Hindu-Muslim riots in his local town of Nagpur. RSS grew into the most powerful and controversial Hindu organization under his successor Madhav Golwalkar, who showed his glowing admiration for Hitler when he wrote, "Germany has shown how well-nigh impossible it is for races and cultures, having differences going to the root, to be assimilated into one united whole, a good lesson for us in Hindustan to learn and profit by." Further writings, however, revealed Golwalkar to be neither a Nazi nor an anti-Semite, though he openly declared that Muslims, Christians, and Communists as enemies of India.

The Vishwa Hindu Parishad or VHP was another Hindu movement that started during this period. It was formed on the principles of reawakening Hindu consciousness and bringing about worldwide cooperation among Hindus. Unlike the RSS or Hindu Mahasabha, VHP had a liberal definition of a Hindu and included not only those born into Hinduism, but anyone willing to believe in the concept of Santana Dharma.

In 1980, the RSS, the VHP, and a number of splinter groups that promoted Hindutva formed the Bharatiya Janata Party or BJP, which became the umbrella organization for Hindu right-wing political activism. Under the leadership of Lal Krishna Advani, the BJP became an all-India nationalist movement, attracting worldwide attention. The BJP soon won the elections and ruled India between 1998 and 2004.

On December 6, 1992, a key incident was to change the meaning of the Hindutva movement forever. It was the day when a mob of about 200,000 Hindu militants tore down Babri Masjid, a 16th century mosque, and attacked other Muslim targets in the northern Indian town of Ayodhya. For years Hindus and Muslims have battled over the site of the Babri Masjid, for the Hindus believe Babri Mosque was built atop the ruins of a temple honoring the Hindu God-Emperor Rama. The public reaction was mixed. Although many think Baber, the Mughal emperor who built the mosque, was an insensitive ruler, most Hindus condemn the razing of the mosque. The Hindutva movement was about preserving the heritage of India, but this act went against the age-old Hindu tradition of showing tolerance and religious maturity.

And this is where my peeve comes from. It is about the recent trend of changing the long-serving Anglicized names of Indian cities to traditional Indian names. Bombay has become Mumbai, Calcutta was changed to Kolkata, and Madras is now Chennai. What concerns me, though, is all the talk of dropping India! After all, it's a foreign name and began with the Greeks[27] and the river Indus. The Greeks have long gone, and so have their successors. The Indus no longer flows through India except for its remote headwaters. So what's next? Bhartiyas in Bharat? I was surprised when I heard that the place Trivandrum in Kerala was changed to the long-sounding Thiruvananthapuram. While many Hindu nationalists commended the appropriateness of the name, many Keraleans felt the change was just a nuisance or represented going back to the dark ages. Were you really trying to be historically accurate or merely settling old scores?

Once of the largest known diamonds in the world, Kohinoor, originally came from Golconda, situated in the Indian state of Andhra Pradesh. Hindu mythology tells us that Lord Krishna adorned this jewel. In its history, Kohinoor had gone through many bitter battles among Indian and Persian rulers and was finally seized as a spoil of war and became part of the British Crown Jewels. If you really want to make your point to the world, I suggest you try getting Kohinoor back. The original Bombites, Calcuttans, Madrasees, Trivandrumites, and the rest of the country will stand up and applaud, for this is more formidable than burning Valentine Day cards or boycotting Western fast foods to uphold Indian tradition ☺.

Now that I have expressed my long-standing peeve against changing names, here's something that's crying out for a change. It is the word "Hindutva" itself. The word has been tainted in recent times and is now

---

27 The etymological roots of "India" come from the Sanskrit word "Sindhu." The sacred text Rig Veda speaks of a land called Sapta-Sindhava, the land of seven rivers. Although five of the seven rivers can still be identified in the province of Punjab, two others—Saraswati and Drasadvati—have long dried up. When the Persians began to penetrate the Indian lands in the sixth century BC, they referred to the modern river Indus and the people living in the region as "Hindu" in old Persian, the cognate of Indic "Sindhu." And when the Macedonians, under Alexander the Great, invaded the same region in the fourth century BC, they used the Greek "Indos" to refer to the river and "India" to the land around and beyond the river.

laden with the ideological overtones of the radical policies of militant Hinduism. There can be no nationalism without involving the Muslims or Christians.

It may be true Indian Muslims celebrate when the Pakistan cricket team wins, but so do the Greeks and Italians in the United States when their homeland wins in soccer. While major wars need to be fought as a united nation, Hindutva has been aimlessly engaged in fighting minor fires and dividing the nation. The movement lacks an outsider's perspective. From the outside, you'll find Indian Muslims and Christians are, after all, Indians. Where else in the world will you find a Vinod Thomas participating in the festivity of Onam or a Christian mother checking the horoscope of her daughter with a Hindu priest. Did it not escape your eye that the Muslim community of India branded the Mumbai terrorists of 2008 not jihadis but fasadis (meaning killers of innocent people) and refused to bury them in the Muslim cemetery? Such is the unique culture of India that the third-largest Muslim country in the world has never produced a single al-Qaeda terrorist. Didn't it occur to you that every Ismail has studied with Gita at school went to college with Vargheese, and lived next door to Ghose? Although at some point in their lives their ancestors took an alternate path to reaching to god, the Indian Christians and Muslims are as much Indianized as any other Hindu and uphold Indian traditions like their counterparts.

What is truly needed is a nationalistic movement that includes all Indians—not just the Hindus, Buddhists, Jains, and Sikhs but also Christians, Muslims, Parsis, and Jews. History has proved that there's no challenge too great for a nation that stands as one. Nationalism can never be achieved by dividing the country on the basis of historical grievances. Nationalism will not be found in the color of fireworks against an inky night sky during Diwali. True nationalism is uniting the multi-religious Indians who live in the blessed land called India irrespective of their caste, color, or creed.

52

Non-Hindus Not Allowed

"One day when I step into the hallway at Guruvayoor temple," sang Jesudas, one of the greatest contemporary singers of South India, "the doors will swing open for me, and I will be blessed with the opportunity to worship Lord Krishna in his divine presence."

Even the gates of heaven may open for the man blessed with a golden voice, but decades after the song was rendered, the doors of Guruvayoor are still closed to Jesudas. Standing between Jesudas and one of the ancient temples of Kerala is a little sign that says, "Non-Hindus not allowed."

Trained in Indian classical music, Jesudas was the music god Hindus never had. Christian by birth, Jesudas identified himself as a Hindu through his devotion to Carnatic music, the roots of which are steeped in the scriptures of Vedas. Such was his devotion to Hindu devotional songs that the Church of Kerala stopped sacramental services to him and threatened him with excommunication.

Called Dwarka of the South, Guruvayoor is among a few temples in India that forbid entry to non-Hindus. Western Hindus who want to visit the temple must show proof of religion. A former president of India, Zail Singh, a turban-wearing Sikh, was denied entry here. Yet Guruvayoor's temple-entry requirements are not as stringent as those of some of the other temples of India. At the famous Jagannath temple at Puri, Orissa, even Hare Krishnas are not allowed. Mahatma Gandhi was denied entry because he was being accompanied by members of the lower caste. Former prime minister Indira Gandhi was prevented from entering the temple because she was married to a Parsi.

Entry to the Guruvayoor temple is controlled by priests and has more to do with tradition than religion, although Hindu priests routinely perform a shuddhi (cleansing) whenever a non-Hindu enters the premises inadvertently. You will be surprised to learn that until the early 1900s, about 40 percent of the Hindus were excluded from entering the temples of Kerala because they belonged to the oppressed castes. The Temple Entry Proclamation of 1936 opened doors to all castes, but it came with a caveat that "certain classes of persons" should not enter the temple at any cost, and the list included drunkards, beggars, and non-Hindus. Over the years, most temples, including Guruvayoor, pruned the long list and merely displayed, "Non-Hindus not allowed!"

But history can be a complicated thing. Landmark decisions that racked up praise and rallied people in one era may appear incredibly short-sighted in a different era. Today the caste system is outlawed and the freedom to worship any deity is a fundamental right of any civilized society.

It's easy to shift blame to the temple priests and accuse them of being the bane of all problems. Although the temple priests never get ahead of the times, they are always pedaling hard to keep up. The chief priest at Guruvayoor insists he is only following centuries-old temple rules, for it's up to the government to change the law.

Historically Hinduism has been mature enough to cop a few blows on its own, for it has continually adapted and evolved over times for its continued existence. Without criticism, there are no reforms. And without reforms, there's no survival. The time has come to honor the long-cherished wish of a self-confessed Christian devotee whose devotional songs are regularly played at the temple premises. The time has arrived for Guruvayoor to dismantle the old wooden doors that opened to a privileged few and to replace them with modern automatic sliding doors[28] that open to everyone regardless of caste or religion.

---

28 OK, not exactly the automatic sliding doors at airports and shopping centers, but you get my point.

Will the government of Kerala take the unprecedented step to legislate temple-entry rights for everyone? Or will it pass the buck to a future generation for fear of a backlash from orthodox Hindus?

While the whole world is watching, moderate Hindus and others will be praying for the day when every devotee in God's own country will have the freedom to worship any god.

53

The Search for Aryans

It's 1942. A military truck crammed with people stops by the side of a road next to a deep ditch. A group of frightened passengers slowly makes its way out of the truck. The silence in the atmosphere is intermittently disrupted by the sound of gunshots. Upon orders by the Nazi gunmen, the group quickly forms into a line. As instructed, the person at the front removes his clothing and places them in a pile, followed by the rest. You can see piles of shoes, underwear, and clothing. An old lady, her hair completely white, is holding a baby in her hands. She is rocking the baby and singing a lullaby, but the baby starts crying aloud. The mother huddles next to her two older daughters while her son seems transfixed by the sight in the ditch. You can see the father holding the hand of his younger son. As the child struggles to hold back tears, the father prays and points to the sky. They are ordered to stand in line next to the ditch in which lies thousands of bodies, some still alive. Holding a tommy gun, an SS man takes aim and peppers bullets from right to left on the helpless people. There are screams everywhere, as they struggle and fall into the ditch. Few moments of thundering silence are broken by the sound of an approaching truck. A new batch of victims has arrived.

(Adapted from an eyewitness account)

More than six million European Jews were killed during the Holocaust as part of a deliberate program of ethnic cleansing of non-

Aryans by the Nazi regime of Germany. Although the word Aryan sometimes refers to the blond-haired, blue-eyed physical ideal of Nazi Germany, it is perhaps the most misunderstood word in the history of mankind.

The word Aryan originally comes from the Vedic scriptures and does not mean a race. It is derived from "Arya," meaning "noble" in Sanskrit and Avestan, the ancient language of the Persians. It is believed that between 1700 BCE and 1400 BCE two groups of people coexisted in what is now eastern Iran and Afghanistan. They were the Avestan and the Rig-Vedic people. Common ties developed between these groups that included composing hymns in praise of gods, worshiping gods using fire rituals, and drinking the juice of a fertility plant called soma. Around 1400 BCE the Rig-Vedic people left Afghanistan and moved into the Indian subcontinent, where the sacred hymns and chants became the early part of Hinduism's Rig Veda. The Avestan people continued to worship their gods, but around 1000 BCE, the visionary and philosopher Zarathushtra carried out a religious revolution, dethroning most of their original gods.

Today historians somewhat loosely call most of the Indo-Iranian speakers Aryans. Modern Iranians also call their country Iran, as the land of the Aryans. Strictly speaking, the word Aryan applied only to the Avestan and Rig-Vedic people because they alone claimed a special status of nobility among all other tribes.

The racial overtones in the meaning, however, had their origins in the 16th century, when linguists observed striking similarities among the Indo-European languages of Latin, Greek, and Sanskrit. Soon it was accepted that all these languages descended from a common source. In the 1800s, the philologist Max Müller named this protolanguage "Aryan" based on what was used by people living in Persia or modern Iran.

It was soon believed that the Aryan language originated with a single Aryan tribe or perhaps an Aryan race. For the next hundred years, language scholars occupied themselves trying to determine where this tribe lived and what they looked like. Initially it was thought that the Aryans were Asians, but the nationalistic European scholars would not accept this theory and began searching for evidence that the Aryans had originated in Europe. German scholars were particularly fascinated with this research and even propounded the idea that the Aryans were a tall, blond, blue-eyed people, whom we would call Nordic today. According to the German scholars and their defenders, the Aryans originally lived next to the Baltic Sea and spread their language and culture throughout the rest of Europe and parts of Asia. The fact that most speakers of Aryan languages did not look at all Nordic was explained away by stating that the original blonds had long since been submerged in the gene pool as a result of the mixing of races.

The shift of meaning that eventually led to the present meaning started in the 1830s, when Friedrich Schlegel, a German scholar, came up with a theory that linked Indo-Iranian words with the German word *Ehre,* "honor," and older Germanic names containing the element *ario.* Schlegel theorized that the word Arya had in fact been what the Indo-Europeans called themselves, meaning "the honorable people." It was widely believed that the Vedic Aryans were ethnically identical to the Goths, Vandals, and other ancient Germanic people.

The idea that the blond Aryans were in fact a superior race was raised explicitly in 1853 by the French aristocrat Joseph Arthur Comte de Gobineau. De Gobineau argued that each race created its own culture, but the mixing of black, white, and yellow races would break cultural barriers and lead to chaos. De Gobineau's ideas became widely popular during this time since it was believed that the Aryan races could prosper as long as they did not allow themselves to be tainted by mixing with the black or yellow races.

Stripped of the scholarly trappings, Aryanism soon influenced the political system and became one of the central tenets of Nazism. The definition of the Aryan ideal also became more detailed. According to one Nazi propaganda poster, "the Aryan is a tall, long-legged, slim. The race is narrow-faced, with a narrow forehead, a narrow high-built nose and a lower jaw and prominent chin, the skin is rosy bright and the blood shines through... the hair is smooth, straight or wavy—possibly curly in childhood. The colour is blond."

Hitler believed that the pure German people, the Aryans, were the master race. One of the reasons, according to Hitler, that Germany lost the First World War was that the German race had been weakened through Aryans marrying non-Aryans. If Germany were to become strong again, the Nazis had to ensure the purity of the Aryan race.

Therefore, the Semitic people, particularly the Jews, came to be seen as a foreign presence within Aryan societies and were blamed for the conversion and destruction of the social order.

With the military defeat of Nazi Germany in 1945 by the Allies, nobody wanted to have anything to do with Aryans and the term was dropped in favor of "Indo-European." In today's English, Aryan, if used at all in scholarly contexts, is normally synonymous with Indo-Iranian. In the United States, the established and less contentious term "Caucasian" became dominant in official usage. Currently, India and Iran are the only countries that use the word Aryan in a demographic denomination. This usage, however, carries no racist connotations.

Although the word Aryan may have disappeared from general usage, the search for the original Aryans or proto-Indo-Europeans still continues.

> *I hope that people will finally come to realize that there is only one race—the human race—and that we are all members of it.*
> – Margaret Atwood (1939–)

54

Swastika

"Swastika is one of the most visually powerful symbols ever devised by mankind," says author Steven Heller. "No other mark—not even variations of the cross or, for that matter, the Nike swoosh—are graphically as powerful as the Swastika. Like most effective symbols, the swastika's geometric purity allows for clarity at any size or distance. When on its axis, the whirling square gives the illusion of movement."

To the East, the swastika is a spiritual sign of long life and good luck. But to the West, it represents death and hatred. How can such a powerful symbol evoke totally opposite emotions on different hemispheres of the world?

The word swastika is a fusion of two Sanskrit words, "su," meaning "good," and "asti" meaning "to exist." The words, when combined, mean "May Good Prevail." It is an ancient sign, used for over three thousand years. Originally a solar symbol, the swastika was anciently associated with Vishnu. Interestingly, the word does not appear in the Vedas, but instead makes its first appearance in the Hindu epics of Ramayana and Mahabharata.

History tells us that the swastika was widely used throughout the world as a symbol of prosperity and good fortune. In India it is the most auspicious symbol among the Hindus and Jains. For Hindus, the swastika is only next to Om in importance. Hindus often decorate the swastika with a dot in each quadrant. In Buddhism, the swastika symbolizes the footprints of Buddha, and in China and Japan, the swastika denotes plurality, prosperity, and long life. The swastika is an ancient symbol and was found in many cultures, including Germany, England, and Greece, although it was known under different names. Even the Native Americans of the United States have long used the symbol.

The shift in the meaning of the swastika came about in the late nineteenth century, when Germany's nationalistic pride began to emerge as countries around it were growing and creating empires. The discovery of objects bearing the swastika in the ruins of Troy (now in modern Turkey) by Heinrich Schliemann seemed to confirm the ancient migration of the Aryans. Schliemann related it with similar shapes found on ancient pots in Germany and concluded that the swastika was a significant religious symbol of their remote ancestors, thereby linking Germanic, Greek, and Indo-Iranian cultures. By the early 20th century, it was used worldwide and was regarded as a symbol of good luck and success.

The swastika was seen as a symbol of the Aryan race, and soon German nationalists began using it to represent Aryan association with Germanic history. The Nazis claimed that the early Aryans of India were the prototypical white invaders and Swastika emerged from the Vedic tradition. The caste system prevalent in India, it was widely believed, originated as a means to avoid racial mixing. The concept of racial purity was an ideology central to Nazism.

In 1920 Adolf Hitler decided that the Nazi party needed its own insignia and flag. A right-facing swastika tilted at forty-five degrees became the national flag and emblem of the Nazi party. Hitler himself is claimed to have personally dictated the precise form of the Nazi swastika. "I myself, meanwhile, after innumerable attempts, had laid down a final form; a flag with a red background, a white disk, and a black swastika in the middle. After long trials I also found a definite proportion between the size of the flag and the size of the white disk, as well as the shape and thickness of the swastika."

Because of its use by Hitler and the Nazis and, in modern times, by neo-Nazis and other hate groups, for many people in the West, the swastika is associated primarily with Nazism and white supremacy. Hence, outside historical contexts, it has become taboo in Western countries. In Germany, a constitutional law prohibits the public display of the swastika, and harsh penalties are imposed.

Despite the taboo of the swastika in the West, millions in the East, including the over two million Indian Americans in the United States, continue to use the swastika as their main religious and cultural symbol. Since the Nazis used the swastika, some cultures are trying to differentiate the two meanings of the swastika by varying its direction. The clockwise, right-facing, Nazi version of the swastika means hate and death while the left-facing version would hold the ancient meaning of the symbol, life and good luck—well, that's only to those who know history. That said, Hindus popularly use the dotted, right-facing swastika, as depicted below.

> *To my mind, the swastika has been irrevocably destroyed as a viable symbol other than Nazi barbarisms. It should be retired with its Nazi trappings intact.*
>
> – Steven Heller

Swastika

55

Aryan Invasion Theory

In September 2002, Tony Blair, then the prime minister of Britain, dropped a bombshell by claiming Iraq had the capability to unleash chemical weapons within forty-five minutes. Shortly thereafter, Colin Powell, the US secretary of state, presented convincing evidence at the United Nations Security Council of an alleged mobile weapons-production facility in Iraq. In the following months, Iraq was invaded, and Saddam Hussein was ousted and hanged. Two years later, the United States abandoned its search for biological and chemical weapons in Iraq. No weapons of mass destruction were ever found. Years later, many questions are still being asked about whether there was a compelling need to go to war despite worldwide protests or evidence to the contrary. The world will never know whether this was an honest mistake or a secret agenda. But one thing is certain: this was not the first time in history such a thing happened.

In the 1800s Winston Churchill used the Aryan Invasion Theory, proposed by Max Müller a few years earlier, as an ideological justification for the British occupation of India. According to this theory, India was invaded and conquered around 1500 BCE by light-skinned nomads from Europe who entered the region through Persia (Iran). These were cattle breeders, the so-called Aryan hordes, who fought from horse-drawn chariots. They overthrew an existing dark-skinned Dravidian civilization and drove them south and imposed their alien culture from which emerged the Hindu culture. The exploits of these nomads were later written down and came to be known as the Rig Veda. Based on this theory, Müller estimated the date of the Rig Veda to be around 1200-1000 BCE.

It is now widely accepted that Müller's dating of the Veda was influenced by his desire to bring Hindu chronology in line with Biblical chronology, for Müller, like many of the loyal Christian missionary scholars of his era, believed the world was created in 4004 BCE. But Müller was also big enough to recognize the dangers of idle speculation that he admitted these were minimum dates. "Whether the Vedic hymns were composed 1000, or 1500, or 2000, or 3000 years BCE, no power on earth will ever determine." Unfortunately, the fine print was overlooked. The theory was reinforced by other scholars, particularly in Europe, and became the accepted history of Hinduism. Most scholars of this period, however, were neither archeologists nor historians in the strict sense. Rather, they were missionaries paid by governments to promote their culture and religion.

It came as no surprise that a theory based on shaky foundations would soon crumble into pieces. The first blow came in the 1920s with the discovery of Indus Valley ruins at Harappa and Mohenjo Daro. Supporters of this theory triumphantly leaped to their feet convinced that these ruins of cities were in fact evidence of a large-scale massacre by the Aryan invaders. The reference in the Rig Veda about the Aryan god Indra destroying hostile people called Dasas was cited as proof. In 1944, when Sir Mortimer Wheeler uncovered skeletal remains at Mohenjo Daro, the skulls were attributed to be those of the last inhabitants of a city that had met its final demise. This was gruesome evidence of butchery beneath the sword, and it attests to the victory of the Aryans.

The finding of a few skeletons over a decade of searching, however, did not provide sufficient evidence of a large-scale attack. The skeletons came from various layers of the ruins suggesting the deaths could have corresponded to different eras, which George Dales, a professor at the University of California–Berkeley, dubbed as a "mythical massacre." Most literary scholars and archeologists today rightly dismiss Wheeler's theory as too simplistic to be valid. Faced with evidence that did not suggest an invasion of any kind, supporters responded by admitting that perhaps it wasn't exactly a large-scale invasion as they envisioned but rather a trickling in or migration of Aryans from the north. The Aryan Invasion Theory then was changed to the Aryan Migration Theory in some quarters.

In the 1980s, proponents of the Aryan Invasion Theory were dealt another blow. Satellite images of the areas located in northwest India and in Pakistan revealed the dry bed of a large extinct river, which could have easily exceeded today's Amazon in size. This was the Saraswati river the Vedas talks about. It flowed from the mountains to the sea, as exactly stated in the Vedas. Earlier it was mistakenly assumed that the Helmand of Afghanistan was the Rig Veda's Saraswati, even though there are no seas in Afghanistan. The Rig Veda places great importance on the river Saraswati since it is said to be the mightiest of the seven rivers and the center of Aryan culture. Whereas the famous River Ganga is mentioned only once, Saraswati is mentioned at least sixty times. Geologists quickly established that the river dried up completely in 1900 BCE, which is at least 400 years before the supposed Aryan migration to India. Because of Saraswati's importance to the Aryan culture, scholars have referred to the Indus Valley Civilization as the Saraswati civilization in recent times.

Most scholars nowadays concur that the decline of the Indus Valley Civilization was due to changes in geographic and climatic conditions. It appears the only Aryan invasion of any kind took place only in the minds of nineteenth-century scholars.

To err is human, and to forgive is divine, but to admit mistakes these days is tantamount to condoning academic ineptness or committing political tomfoolery. In the West, proponents of the Iraq war continue to insist weapons of mass destruction will eventually be found. In the East, new discoveries are being reported. With fresh evidence emerging, the absurdity of the Aryan Invasion Theory is becoming even more apparent. So long as Max Müller continues to remain the spiritual leader of the academics, the notion of nomadic Aryans invading the locals will be perpetuated in textbooks and literary works. If you truly believe a barbaric horde of nomadic tribes descended upon India in horse-drawn chariots, swinging swords and singing paeans of God, you need a friend to throw cold water on your face. Someone needs to wake you up from dreaming.

> *I am convinced that everything has come down to us from the banks of the Ganges, astronomy, astrology, metempsychosis, etc...It does not behove us, who were only savages and barbarians when these Indian and Chinese peoples were civilized and learned, to dispute their antiquity.*
>
> – Voltaire (1694–1778)

56

A Salute to Vamadeva Shastri

In the 1990s, Pandit Vamadeva Shastri stunned the world with his discovery that would change our view of the history of ancient India. With newly uncovered archeological evidence, he demonstrated that the centuries-old Aryan Invasion Theory and its variants were plainly wrong. The reaction was predictable. While many archeologists and Indian scholars regarded the discovery as groundbreaking, most Western scholars around the world were unanimous in condemning his theory.

The key evidence for Shastri was the satellite images in the area around Punjab that clearly unveiled the existence of the dried-up bed of the river Saraswati mentioned in the Vedas. Geologists quickly established that this river, which once traversed through what is now the Thar Desert, dried up around 1900 BCE. The images further revealed that the numerous sites discovered alongside Harappa, Mohenjo Daro, and Mehrgarh were together once part of a civilization that thrived on the banks of river Saraswati, and not the Indus as originally thought. From the 1980s, there were definite signs uncovered to show that the civilization of ancient India was much older and continuous, but it was Shastri, with the help of colleagues, who put it all together and beat everyone to the punch.

The evidence is irrefutable, undeniable, and conclusive. It walks like a duck. It squawks like a duck. But why is everyone not calling it a duck? Was Shastri a visionary far too ahead of his time or is the academic world still in awe of the formidable authority of Max Müller, who himself expressed reservation at his dating of the Vedas. It appears that the religion of "Europe as the cradle of civilization" is so deeply ingrained among the contemporary scholars that they will do virtually anything to justify their continued belief in it.

Since the publication of Shastri's theory, plenty of energetic crusaders have come forward writing highly intellectual, multipage discourses concerning everything wrong with the theory. Most criticisms were personal attacks on Shastri questioning just about everything, from his knowledge of Sanskrit and his astronomical sense to his background in Ayurveda. These criticisms raise important questions less on the ancient civilization of India and more on the inflexibility of scholars trapped in denial. Almost inevitably, the use of flawed linguistic arguments will find its way to defend the archeologically unsustainable theories of the past. Don't get me wrong. Linguistic reconstructions are useful when limited to certain generalizations, but the fact is they are purely hypothetical. With a bit of ingenuity anything can be proved or disproved.

Then there are a slew of silly objections based on lack of clarity. "The satellite images are not clear." "The horse bones don't reveal real horses." And there have been attempts at stretching old theories to fit newly uncovered data. The Rig Veda has more than 150 references of the Sanskrit word Samudra. In Sanskrit and in Indian languages with roots to it, this word means ocean and nothing else, yet critics make the claim that Samudra refers to something else. I've been there before. Such petty objections say more than what is being told. People will accept another theory only if it fits into their reality of a universe created around 4000 BCE.

Shastri has further debunked the Aryan Invasion Theory by attempting to date the Vedic culture. The Rig Vedians were a sophisticated kind of people and used the Vedic calendar, which is based on astronomical sightings of the equinoxes and solstices. According to Shastri, the Yajur Veda and the Atharva Veda have several references to a summer solstice and vernal equinox, which, when extrapolated, points to a date of 2400 BCE and years prior to that. This dating precedes Max Müller's dating of the Vedas by at least a thousand years. So far, critics remain largely ignorant or overwhelmingly silent on this topic.

Of all the things Shastri has written, I am most intrigued by his observation that there's no difference between south Indians and north Indians. In fact, recent DNA evidence readily confirms this theory. According to Shastri, the British created the idea of India as a land of two races: the lighter-skinned Aryans of the north and the darker-skinned Dravidians of the south. The British view was that the original inhabitants of India were the Dravidians, whom the invading Aryans conquered and drove to the south. Much of what we call Hindu culture today was in fact the early Dravidian culture, according to the British. The problem with the British version of history is that none of the ancient manuscripts of northern Indians ever mention any such thing as having driven the Dravidians out of north India. The Dravidians have no memory of ever having lived in north India. In fact, the traditions of south Indians suggest that their forebears came from the south itself.

Ancient India is the birthplace of yoga, the abode of the mightiest mountains, home to the once greatest river of the world, seat to highly developed literature and intellectual insights, the original home to many major religions of this planet, the country that produced the greatest languages of the world, and the birthplace of a billion Indians who allow Western scholars to interpret their history for them. According to Shastri, Indians can blame no one but themselves for the misinterpretation of their own culture, for universities in India routinely using Western history books and Vedic translations of missionary scholars like Max Müller, Griffith, and Monier Williams[29].

If you believe history will be delivered to you in a silver platter, you will be bitterly disappointed. The vision of the Vedas came not from the academic corridors of Oxford or Harvard but from sages living in ancient India who set their mind on revealing the truth. The ancient wisdom is best understood by those who have true appreciation for the religious and spiritual traditions of India. If you truly believe you are the descendant of the noble ones called Aryans, then start acting like

---

29 Monier Williams and Max Müller were contemporaries at Oxford University and at one point competed for professorship for which they had to affirm their support for Christian evangelization in India. Born in Bombay, India, Williams was seen as a less brilliant scholar than Müller, but had more practical knowledge of religious practices of Hinduism. Müller, in contrast, never visited India. In his published work, the conservative Monier Williams predicted the demise of the Hindu religion and called for Christian evangelism to ward off the spread of Islam.

one, for you'll need to do more than just burning effigies or organizing hartals.

For an India steeped in rituals and traditions, it would take a cultural shift to realize that only a critical mind, not a subservient mind, will lead to the development of genuine scholarship. Until that happens, it will be the Western-educated men and women who will interpret, misinterpret, and later reinterpret our own history for us. Thus it took a Western-educated Indian called Gandhi many years to liberate India from the clutches of British rule. About fifty years later, it took another Western-born and Western-educated American Catholic called David Frawley, aka Pandit Vamadeva Shastri, to liberate India from its misinterpreted history. If Gandhi was the father of the modern nation of India, then Shastri was surely the guardian of Vedic India, for there's no one who has done so much to correct India's misinterpreted past.

> *All truth passes through three stages. First, it is ridiculed. Second, it is violently opposed. Third, it is accepted as being self-evident.*
> – Arthur Schopenhauer (1788–1860)

57

The Milk Miracle

It's September 21, 1995. Anila Premji holds a teaspoonful of milk next to the mouth of a lifeless idol of Ganesha, the elephant-headed god of wisdom. The milk disappears. Stunned, she brings a second teaspoonful of milk close to the idol's trunk. In seconds, it disappears too. Said Anila, "To me it was a miracle. It gave me a sense of feeling that there is a god, a sense of spirit on this earth."

Hours before Anila fed milk to her favorite deity, an ordinary man in New Delhi, India, had an extraordinary dream in which he dreamt that Ganesha craved for a little milk. Upon awakening, he headed to the nearest temple, where he offered a spoonful of milk to a small stone image of Ganesha. To his astonishment, the milk disappeared. Word of the event spread like wildfire and by mid-morning, as millions flocked to the temples, statues of the entire Hindu pantheon all over India were found consuming milk. Twenty-four hours later, just as quickly as the phenomenon took off in India, it came to a complete stop. But the worldwide milk miracle was beginning elsewhere, as news spread beyond India. The phenomenon was soon observed in Hindu temples in Britain, Canada, Dubai, and Nepal. Never before in history had such a miracle happened simultaneously on a global scale.

Once the miracle spread worldwide, leading national papers, such as the _New York Times_, the _Washington Post_, and the _Financial Times_ in the United Kingdom, picked up the story. Television, radio, and newspapers eagerly covered this phenomenon, as skeptical journalists held their milk-filled spoons to the gods—and watched the milk disappear. "As a lapsed Catholic, I don't believe in stories of the Virgin Mary shedding tears. Indeed, I would say I was as skeptical as anyone—but it's difficult to dismiss something you have seen for yourself," so wrote a journalist in a leading foreign daily.

While the foreign press gave a warm reception to this worldwide phenomenon, the Indian press, on the contrary, showed scant respect and dismissed it as a form of mass insanity with headlines like "People go Berserk at Milk Miracle" and "Milk-Drinking Deities Unleash Mass Hysteria." Editorials in Indian newspapers claimed that this was a plot by the Hindu fundamentalists to win the next elections. A good deal of milk was being wasted, they pointed out, blatantly choosing to ignore the significance of the event.

Soon an eminent team of scientists from India's Ministry of Science and Technology arrived at the scene to explain the phenomenon. After careful analysis, they concluded that the milk was not absorbed by the statue, but rather deposited as a thin layer of droplet by capillary action. The scientists then proceeded to demonstrate this on TV by placing green powder in the milk and showing the face of the statue becoming green. Surface tension and capillary action, coupled with mass hysteria, was the official explanation, which seemed to satisfy the scientific types.

Then started the war of the faiths—the scientific faith versus the religious faith—which continues to this day. For believers, an explanation was unnecessary, but the nonbelievers need answers. For a believer, a miracle is a marvelous event of a divine nature—the impossible becoming possible. For a nonbeliever, it is an event of low probability bound to happen from time to time. When an event that defies logic or science happens, believers see the fingerprints of god. Nonbelievers, however, turn themselves into knights in search of the Holy Grail of scientific truth.

The postmortem began with, first, the veiled mocking. "The Hindus are a weird lot to worship idols. How in the world can idols drink milk? You see, Mickey Mouse drank a spoonful of milk like those statues, so Mickey Mouse should be inducted into the Hindu pantheon."

Then there were attempts at ridiculing the event after watching a few homemade Internet videos. With milk running down the statue and all around the base like a sink, skeptics were quick to conclude that devotees were tipping the spoonful of milk on the statue and shouting "Eureka! It's a miracle!" According to a few, the milk all around the base of the idol was perhaps due to the statue "drinking milk and urinating later." The fact that when thousands of people feed with excited hands it is statistically inevitable some milk would spill was lost on these skeptical folks.

Finally, an attempt was made at an explanation using capillary action and surface tension. "A plaster statue of Lyndon Johnson [former president of the United States] will do exactly the same, perhaps with a pint of beer. It's all about physics and science."

Whatever your beliefs and opinions, this was undoubtedly the best documented paranormal phenomenon of modern times. Many idols that drank milk on that particular day refused to consume in the future. If the milk miracle was because of capillary action, then what happened to capillary action on other days? If the milk miracle was a case of fooling some of the people some of the time, then what happened when the phenomenon was observed worldwide with eminent journalists and scientists themselves validating its authenticity.

Forget surface tension and capillary action. Science is still scratching its head for genuine answers.

❖ ❖ ❖

58

Pseudo-Psychoanalysis of Ganesha

Ganesha, the most popular god in the Hindu pantheon, the son of Shiva and Parvati, is depicted as an elephant head mounted on a human body with a protruding belly and a curved trunk, which, according to professor Paul Courtright, an American academic, represents a "limp phallus," much to the outrage of millions of Ganesha devotees.

Courtright perhaps never knew much about elephants. Those who have seen one will tell you an elephant's trunk is like the Swiss army knife of animal appendages. It is strong enough to uproot a tree yet flexible enough to lift a needle off the ground. With its trunk, the elephant can collect gallons of water for a shower, pluck the leaves off a tree for a snack, or even sprinkle dust on its body to protect from fleas.

Hindus compare the elephant's trunk to the human mind. Like the elephant's trunk, the mind should be strong enough to face the ups and downs of the external world yet delicate enough to explore the subtle realms of the inner world. But Courtright wasn't finished. Using Freudian psychoanalysis, he interpreted Ganesha to a eunuch employed to guard the women of the harem. According to Courtright, the broken tusk and displaced head are symbols of castration. Ganesha's appetite for sweets was seen as a sign of sexual longing. You see, Courtright was attacking the religion and its age-old beliefs and traditions.

It has long been known to psychologists that psychoanalysis of mythical figures is loaded with problems, with conclusions ranging from the trivial to the outrageous. Classical psychoanalysis itself has been discredited in the psychology literature and is a dying field, while culture-sensitive, cognitive, and integrative theories are becoming more popular. The Freudian theory of psychoanalysis has excessive theoretical baggage without evidence. To apply it to a religious myth is like applying one myth to explain another myth.

To illustrate the absurdity of Courtright's interpretation, Vishal Agrawal, a Hindu scholar, applied Courtright's analyses to a televised scene of an elephant raising its trunk to salute the arrival of Acharya Jayendra Saraswati. The saint, on receiving the warm welcome, approaches the animal and pats the lowered trunk in approval. Since the non-raised trunk of Ganesha represents a flaccid penis for Courtright, the raised trunk, using Courtright's interpretation, can be interpreted as an erect phallus. The patting of the trunk by the Acharya can be viewed as castration of the animal. Moreover, the lowering of the trunk can be seen as the triumph of asceticism over eroticism.

While Hindus all over the world protested against cultural vandalism, colleagues and friends of Courtright came to his rescue by writing frivolous essays expounding the virtues of academic freedom and free speech. Although Courtright's limp interpretation tickled many in academia, it raises serious questions about overall balance between academic integrity and freedom of speech. Will the psychoanalysis of Prophet Mohammed's relationship with his nine-year-old wife Ayesha be considered genuine scholarship? Or will the psychoanalysis of an anxious Joseph faced with his virgin wife Mary giving birth to baby Jesus be regarded as a triumph of academic freedom?

Millions of Hindus, Buddhists, and Jains worship Ganesha in their everyday life as an endearing god, but all Courtright could see was penis envy, castration anxiety, cathexis, and repression. Hindu jihadists haven't been born yet. Energetic crusaders ready to denounce the blasphemous writings of their gods and goddesses haven't arrived in Hinduism. Does that mean every Wendy, Sarah, and Jeffrey can have a crack at the age-old Hindu beliefs in their own perverse ways in the name of academic freedom?

There is a fine line between cultural sensitivity and academic freedom. Like acrobats on a high wire, the writer who balances on this line is also the one who knows how to interpret and present other cultures in their own light. Academic freedom was merely reduced to an expression of sexual fantasy in Courtright's work. This revives the longstanding debate on whether mocking the cherished beliefs of other religions deserves protection by the First Amendment of the United States.

The Freudian interpretation of Ganesha reveals more about the author and less about the religion. While such crass misinterpretations may occasionally see the light of the day, Ganesha will remain dearest in the hearts of millions of Hindus.

> *Many people die at twenty five and aren't buried until they are seventy five.*
>
> – Benjamin Franklin (1706–1790)

59

Holy Queen of Sleaze

In 2002, a worldwide movement of unearthing scandalous academic work started as a mass online protest to counter the relentless negative portrayal of Hinduism in the academic world. It was also the day Indians all over the world and like-minded Westerners came together in a show of strength against increasing academic misrepresentations. The seeds of this movement were planted by Rajiv Malhotra in his 2002 classic essay entitled "Wendy's Child Syndrome," in which Malhotra exposes four renowned scholars of RISA (Religions In South Asia), headed by Wendy Doniger, and their flawed techniques often used in the negative portrayal of Indic studies and Hinduism.

While some think of Doniger as the czarina of Hinduism studies, others regard her as the holy queen of sleaze. But to her students, she is the one that can make or break careers. Wendy is a member of many prestigious academic organizations and her works are extensively quoted in most books on Hinduism, including this one (yes, give credit where it is due). Not only has she given more students their PhDs in Hinduism than any other professor, she has also successfully placed her former students in many top academic jobs throughout the Western world. "There is no place one can go to in this academic discipline," writes Malhotra, "without running into the effect of her influence, through her large cult of students, who glorify her in exchange for her mentorship."

Doniger's predilection for the sleaze is well-documented, as can be seen in this introduction: "Professor Wendy Doniger is known for being rude, crude and very lewd in the hallowed portals of Sanskrit Academics. All her special works have revolved around the subject of sex in Sanskrit texts..." Others note that although Doniger has written extensively about Hinduism, her works, suffer from a notable lack of passion. About Hinduism, Doniger writes, "The Bhagavad Gita is not as nice a book as some Americans think...Throughout the Mahabharata ... Krishna goads human beings into all sorts of murderous and self-destructive behaviors such as war.... The Gita is a dishonest book ..."

Like her character, her knowledge sometimes comes under a cloud. Some suspect her Sanskrit isn't any good for a professor teaching Hinduism. A Harvard University professor, Michael Witzel says, "Wendy's rendering of even the first two paadas of the Rig Veda is more of a translation, and her style is rather a stream of unconnected George Bush-like anacoluthas." Citing Witzel's critical assessment, Malhotra concludes that "this is as audacious as saying the Pope is not a good Catholic."

As for Doniger, she makes no excuses for her style when she writes, "Aldous Huxley once said that an intellectual was someone who had found something more interesting than sex; in Indology, an intellectual need not make that choice at all."

Doniger is known to be obsessed with the obscene, but that's okay—well, no one should complain about the personal preferences of yours and mine. For some time, Doniger has been masquerading psychoanalysis as genuine scholarship. Under the guise of objective analysis, she has patented a brand of psychoanalysis that she and her disciples misapply to nonliving religious figures, manipulating texts, ignoring sources, and manufacturing dirt where none exists. And this is what many complain about.

Western psychologists do not regard Freudian methods of psychoanalysis as solid proofs of anything serious. Freud himself forbids the use of his techniques against people who are not living anymore. Moreover, the validity of the theory is lost when applied in a non-Western context. The Hindu philosopher Aurobindo notes, "One cannot discover the meaning of the lotus by analyzing the secrets of the mud in which it grows." Most people, however, realize the dangers of applying psychoanalysis to religious figures only when they see such revolting misrepresentations find their way into the shelves of libraries and become prescribed textbooks for students.

The world would've been a much better place had such bogus works been purged from the libraries and other institutions of the world. But these weapons of mass instruction will continue to remain so in the name of academic freedom, critical views, or an outsider's perspective.

So far I have only scratched the surface of Hinduism bashing. We have more rogue academics to deal with.

> *Nothing convinces me we are deep into Kali Yuga, the dark ages of Hinduism, than the works of Wendy Doniger.*
> – Swami Achuthananda

So much unwarranted criticism of a distinguished professor, right? Peruse the customer reviews of books by Wendy Doniger on Amazon, and you will understand what I mean.

60

My Karma Ran Over Your Dogma

> _Rules are not necessarily sacred, principles are._
> – Franklin D. Roosevelt (1882–1945)

About 400 years ago, Galileo observed that the earth orbited the sun and not the other way around. He was excommunicated and placed under house arrest. That the sun revolved around the earth was the view of many churchmen of his time.

About 250 years later, Charles Darwin proclaimed that species evolved through mutation and natural selection. He was condemned because the theory of evolution contradicted the Christian belief that all living things were created at the same time.

Both Darwin and Galileo were unfortunate victims of the religious dogma of their times. So what is religious dogma? It is the unshaken belief within a religion that something is true regardless of proof. Held as authoritative and indisputable, dogma is something that should never be violated. Detractors are shunned or expelled from the religious group.

Found in Western religions like Christianity, Islam, and Judaism, dogmas form the core beliefs that must be upheld at all times. It is commonly associated with the Roman Catholic tradition. Since dogma is based on unproven beliefs, it inevitably leads to discord and conflict within the religion.

Historically, religions fiercely resisted attacks on dogma. With the advancement of science, however, religions also had a need to coexist for survival and growth. Societies need religion to provide meaning and cohesion, but they also need tolerance and creativity to progress. It was for these reasons Galileo's excommunication for the heresy was revoked by the late 20th century. A century and a half after Darwin's findings, Pope admitted that evolution was not contradictory to religious beliefs.

Hindus' believe dogma, which by its very nature, is an assertion of ignorance. Beliefs are influenced by time, place, and a myriad of circumstantial variables that cannot be reduced to a single formula or coded into a fundamental truth. Dogma shuts the door to a deeper perception. The human objective is to understand the nature of the world by using all means at our disposal without creating barriers of definitions. According to Max Weber, German philosopher of the 20th century, nothing can be taken for granted or is generally accepted in Hinduism, not even the doctrine of karma.

Western religions are founded on dogmas, Eastern religions on principles like karma. Dogma is a product of short-term thinking, whereas karma is the result of timeless wisdom. The rules that underpin dogma will work as long as circumstances remain constant. It is when circumstances change that you'll hear people say, "My karma ran over your dogma," meaning the negative karma accrued by the actions has come to haunt narrow dogmatic rules.

Rules control behavior, but principles guide them. Rules will change with circumstances, but principles remain constant forever. Wisdom doesn't inhabit a set of rules but in the ongoing application of the principles.

All religions strive to promote peace, but dogma breaks them apart. It is not religions but religious dogmas that create wars.

Rules are written for the obedience of fools and the guidance of wise men.

–Anonymous

No religion which is narrow and which cannot satisfy the test of reason, will survive the coming reconstruction of society in which the values will have changed and character, not possession of wealth, title or birth will be the test of merit.

– Mahatma Gandhi (1869–1948)

61

Shady Professor Shoddy Scholarship

The Irish playwright and critic Bernard Shaw once said, "He who can, does. He who cannot, teaches." Shaw was perhaps being playful, but those who pursue teaching as a career in religious studies occasionally engage their personal experiences and prejudices under the guise of objective analysis in what is commonly known as Hinduism bashing. Okay, it's only a few that muddy the esteemed institution of religious studies, but this fast-growing discipline has now become the battleground where religious warfare is fought using academic weapons of mass destruction known as psychoanalysis. In his widely acclaimed essay titled "Wendy's Child Syndrome," Rajiv Malhotra exposes the incestuous cult at RISA (Religions In South Asia) and identifies four renowned scholars led by Wendy Doniger. We have discussed at length Doniger's modus operandi in an earlier chapter. Now we turn our attention to one of her students, Jeffrey Kripal, and his works.

With an unmistakable Indian last name, Kripal is a Roma, the wandering gypsies originally from India but nowadays found throughout the world. The Roma, whose population today is estimated at twenty-five million, were initially believed to have been from Egypt until scholars in the late eighteenth century found clear linguistic evidence linking them to Hindu ancestry.

As an ambitious young man, Kripal was striving to become a Christian monk, but midway he turned his attention toward Hinduism. Seeing

191

tolerance in Hinduism as a weakness not a strength, Kripal bit the very hand that rocked the cradle of his forebears for many centuries. The 19th century Hindu saint Ramakrishna, much revered in Bengal and in many parts of the world, was reduced to a sexually abused homosexual molesting children, including Vivekananda, his protégé. The mystical experiences of Ramakrishna, according to Kripal, were nothing but pathological sexual conditions requiring further psychoanalytic investigation.

Among the first to leap to their feet and congratulate Kripal was none other than his mentor Wendy Doniger. With her influence, Kripal won the book award for the American Academy of Religion (AAR), a job at Harvard, and a prestigious position at Rice University. Among the books cited to learn about Ramakrishna, notes Malhotra, *Encyclopedia Britannica* listed Kripal's work as the top choice.

Kripal accomplished all these without knowing a single word of Bengali or having adequate training in Sanskrit or exposure to the Bengali culture—key requirements for psychoanalysis, which by itself renders his book a bogus work. The academics that bestowed the highest award on Kripal seem to have been sleeping at the wheel, for sweeping judgments on Ramakrishna and Hinduism were passed without any peer review or academic due process. Truth and credibility are no longer the criteria for judging scholarly articles, for it appears that the more the scholarly dirt you manufacture, the higher you advance in religious studies. When Swami Tyagananda of the Ramakrishna Order presented his 130-page rebuttal listing serious factual errors, suddenly questions were raised about Kripal's work.

Like a child caught with his hand in the cookie jar, Kripal showed the annoyance of someone never used to interrogation. "You haven't read my book!" In academic style, he brushed aside criticism by labeling them ad hominem attacks. Then the denial "I didn't mean that … but I meant that …," followed by dancing and waffling, before beating a retreat. The truth is you can wrap yourself in the comfort of academic protocols only to a certain extent, but with 91 factual errors and errata as thick as the Oxford dictionary, Kripal was fooling no one but himself. The door of opportunity soon opened for the sheltered university man with a golden chance to come clean on his writings in the form of an invitation to defend his theory in a debate. Unfortunately Kripal declined the request, making him look like a shady professor peddling shoddy work.

While people of all cultures see a mother's lap as a place of affection, Kripal saw only "genitals" or "a defiled sexual space." The human head became a phallus, and an affectionate pat on a child, an act of sodomy. Had Kripal psychoanalyzed Abraham Lincoln, Mother Teresa or Buddha using his methodology, he would have painted them as a bunch of homosexuals suffering from pathological sexual conditions. Was Kripal narrating his own childhood experience through his work on Ramakrishna? Did his insecurities as a Roma (half-Roma, to be precise) and his own self-acknowledged homophobia become the driving force in his work?

Paradoxically, the work of Jeffrey Kripal reveals little about Ramakrishna but provides deeper insights into the cult of scholars afflicted with the disease called Wendy's Child Syndrome. As Malhotra notes, it is quite common for Western scholars to unleash their insecurities and play out their private lives through their analyses about people in ways that are both positive and negative. In Kripal's writings, all that was on display was the sordid aspects of his own personal life experiences.

As we last know, Kripal has moved on to a new space and a new place, yet there is no guarantee history will not be repeated. Sooner or later, someone on the fast road to fame will pick a renowned Hindu saint of yesteryears and pen his memoirs dressed up as genuine scholarship. Next we know is that an academic of higher standing but afflicted with Wendy's Syndrome will stamp his or her approval by bestowing the highest honor on the scandalous work.

There's no doubt Kripal has permanently scarred the sacred image of Ramakrishna. The choice to remain a silent spectator is not an option, for it behooves upon the leaders of RISA to restore the legacy of the Bengali saint. Millions of devotees of Ramakrishna look forward to the day when the sanctity of their saint is vindicated from baseless allegations. Genuine scholarship will trump the day when the University of Chicago owns up to its mistake and boldly rescinds the PhD awarded for bogus work.

Think this is a pipe dream? I don't think so. Freedom from the British for what is now the nation of India was once thought to be a pipe dream. Anything less falls short.

> *Evidence from the past decades shows that the history of Hinduism is markedly different from what is generally believed or taught in classrooms. The finger of blame for making Hinduism inaccessible to the world should point squarely at the academics at high places.*
>
> – Swami Achuthananda

62

Amba and Sarah

With its lush green fields, shimmering lakes, serene beaches, tranquil backwaters, and above all hospitable people, Kerala makes you wonder whether the land famously known as "God's own country" is indeed the place called heaven. Yet while I was away from Kerala, a Westerner called Sarah sneaked into the small southern Indian state, observed its age-old traditions by establishing trusting relationships with some men in Kerala, and followed up with this absurd conclusion that homosexuality was running rampant in "God's own queer country," implying, in no uncertain terms, that the Gods themselves were gays.

Please welcome another reckless academic from RISA (Religions of South Asia), for Sarah Caldwell, as noted by Rajiv Malhotra, is afflicted with Wendy's Child Syndrome. To get an idea of Sarah's writings, you don't have to delve much deeper than browse the titles of her works. For her recent work entitled "The Bloodthirsty Tongue and Self-feeding Breast: Homosexual Fellatio Fantasy in a South Indian Ritual Tradition," she was bestowed the prestigious Robert Stoller Award, not for the length of the title or its revealing nature but for her scholarship on the Hindu Goddess, which validates my empirical findings that the more the scholarly dirt you can manufacture, the higher you advance in religious studies.

There's something about Caldwell's pet theories that whenever she puts them to paper, critics in hordes are attracted to her work. One of them, Cynthia Humes, a former professor of religious studies in the United States, wrote the following after reviewing Caldwell's work: "*Caldwell documents numerous themes of sexuality, abuse, and vengeance in Keralite religion and culture. She concludes, 'Mutiyettu actors who are particularly talented at playing the role of Kali might be traumatized individuals whose particular psychological propensities and histories compel them towards this form of performance' (259). I find this unconvincing. As she herself notes, Caldwell did not conduct a detailed study of or even collect the life histories of the individual Mutiyettu actors playing the role of Kali; so there is no direct evidence of even one individual fitting this typology*" (259).

When confronted with criticism, Caldwell made a sweeping generalization that the Hindu community as such suffers from psychological disorder but then backtracked by confessing that it was the product of her academic training in psychoanalysis.

Now Caldwell is among the elite in RISA and wields the power to decide which papers or topics get included at academic conferences on Hinduism. You would be surprised to learn she's a Hindu after all, having converted to the religion many decades ago. Why would a devout Hindu, as she claims she is, who regularly practices yoga and considers Hinduism and India to be the riches of one of the greatest civilizations, publish offensive statements about Hinduism?

The answer can be found in these writings of a Hindu girl called Amba.

"*Just prior to joining the ashram, I had suffered serious psychological distress due to a series of abusive incestuous contacts with male family members that had culminated in my leaving Yale University suddenly in my sophomore year … My background of sexual abuse, which I certainly could not have recognized or named at that time, added dimensions of fear, mistrust, and denial to the heady mix. The discovery of the 'left-handed' sexual practices of Kaula Tantrism through the Abhinavagupta volume held out a new path from any I had yet seen.*"

…

"My guru was Swami Muktananda, that I gave him my whole heart and soul, that he taught me everything of ultimate value that I know, that I can never express the depth of the love and insight I gained in his presence."

...

"I had left the ashram with a muddled sense of erotic mystery and unknown, unspoken, secret powers. It took many more years for this heady mix to percolate with my own buried experiences of incestuous sexual abuse, which finally forced themselves into the light of day. Through intensive psychoanalysis, I was able to think through the odd conjunctions of Tantric symbolism, buried pain, and ecstatic devotion, attempting to sort out and synthesize these diverse currents. When I learned through the personal testimony of friends that Baba had in fact performed these strange actions, I was disgusted and repelled. I no longer could regard him as my guru, no longer could see anything positive in the experiences I had during those long years."

According to Malhotra, the projection of a scholar's personal psychosis upon the subject or research by filtering the sources and stretching the facts is the very definition of Wendy's Child Syndrome. Caldwell's writings can be seen as an autobiography of a traumatized Western feminist struggling with feelings of guilt and inadequacy.

The traumatized victims start out as misfits in their own society and find solace and meaning in Hinduism. Later in life, they make a complete reversal upon realizing the existence of a lucrative market for their stories, rejecting the culture that gave them a dignified life. Sarah Caldwell and Jeffrey Kripal are mere examples of this phenomenon. Their stories have meaning only in their individual lives.

In case it wasn't obvious, Amba was the Hindu name adopted by Sarah Caldwell.

63

Chakras – Determining Your Nature

Shiva Linga, the most popular icon of Lord Shiva, is a rounded, elliptical stone set on a circular base. Shiva Linga represents Shiva's symbol, since Linga means "symbol" in Sanskrit, among other things. Citing the Vedas (Atharva-Veda Samhita) back in 1900, Swami Vivekananda stated that Shiva Linga represents the eternal Brahman and nothing else. Yet scholars from far and near associate Linga with the phallus and the circular base with the vagina, thereby linking worship of Shiva Linga to the worship of the generative power of nature.

Why do some people see the image of God in Shiva Linga while others see it as a symbol of sex? People are an interesting lot, to say the least. They are the same types who see sexual symbolism in the spire and font of a Christian church, while others extrapolate no such connection.

The apparent contradiction in perspectives did not escape the eye of Rajiv Malhotra. In his eminently readable essay entitled "Wendy's Child Syndrome," Malhotra applied the Hindu Chakra System to explain the differing perspectives for the same thing. Although the Hindu Chakra is a seven-level system, it can be broadly categorized into two: the lower Chakras and the higher Chakras.

The lower Chakras correspond to the first three Chakras and represent basic animal instincts. The first (and the lowest) chakra is located near the anus and is about survival. The second Chakra, near the genitals, represents procreation, while the third, located near the navel, is about power and position.

The higher Chakras correspond to levels four, five, and six and represent higher qualities, such as compassion, altruism, creativity, intuition, etc. The highest Chakra, or the crown Chakra, represents moksha.

According to Malhotra, a person's mental state determines his perspective at each level of Chakra. When an experience is interpreted at a certain level in the hierarchy, it gets translated into a perspective corresponding to that Chakra.

Malhotra drives home this point using as examples the cult of scholars afflicted with Wendy's Child Syndrome, who, according to him, reside at the lowest two chakras in their scholarship. These scholars interpreted religious experience through the prism of their own life experiences. Jeffrey Kripal saw Hinduism from the anal perspective in keeping with his own homophobia and insecurities about his Roma heritage, while Doniger and Caldwell flip-flopped between the anal and genital Chakras, resulting in crude and lewd depictions of Hinduism.

Yet not all RISA (Religions In South Asia) scholars viewed Hinduism from the lowest Chakras. In Malhotra's account, Father Clooney, Chris Chapple, Ian Wicher, Edwin Bryant, and many others looked at Hinduism from the middle chakras by examining practices like bhakti, compassion in terms of spiritual advancement. They came away with a far deeper understanding of the religious practices of Hinduism.

While many view religious experience through their own life experiences, others force themselves to see things from the lower Chakras. I say this because there is a trend in modern academic circles, particularly among Western writers, to treat concepts like altruism and consciousness as too idealistic and vague. These writers fear to explore beyond their narrow realms. Clinging tightly in the security of the lower Chakras, they deny the existence of that which cannot be tested, proven, or measured. Religious experience like consciousness has been narrowly attributed to the effects of trauma, colonialism, projection, or a lack of general understanding.

Malhotra further traces the history of Western psychology using the Chakra system. According to Malhotra, Freud was obsessed with depicting everything in terms of sexual anomalies and spent his entire life stuck at the anal and genital Chakras. Carl Jung, on the other hand, researched Hinduism extensively and practiced yoga based on Patanjali's texts. Operating at the middle Chakras, Jung was able to break away from Freud and spiritualize Western science. Among the contemporary psychologists, Ken Wilbur, after decades of studying Sri Aurobindo, Tantra, and Kashmir Shaivism, is among a few who operates at the highest Chakra and understands the non-dual state.

The truth is Linga has more than a dozen meanings in Sanskrit, but which Chakra will you use to decipher its meaning? Are you hopelessly stuck in the security of lower levels and view it as a phallic symbol? Or are you ready to elevate yourself from the base levels and worship it as a symbol of God?

When you transcend your basic instincts and reach the higher levels, you will inherit the vision of people like George Harrison, Sivaya Subramuniyaswami, and Vamadeva Shastri. Then you will see Hinduism in an entirely different light that is so magnificent, majestic, and mind-boggling.

> *If the only tool you have is a hammer, you tend to see every problem as a nail.*
>
> – Abraham Maslow (1908–1970)

Shiva Linga

64

Inglish

Let's play a game. It's called "Repeat The Word." You and I are the contestants. Here are the rules. You say a word in English, and if I repeat it correctly, I get a point. Next, I say a word in Hindi and if you can repeat it right, you get a point. My turn first. The word is "Khoobsoorat."[30]

Think it's not fair? With English as your first language, you can't make the vocal maneuvers required of other languages? When you have difficulty saying Hindi words, why are you moaning that Indian English lowers the class and dignity of spoken English. Did it not occur to you when you hired Indian workers that they weren't exactly known to speak in the Queen's English?

Believe me, I know Indian words like Namaste and Tamasha do not roll out from your Western tongue with the ease of a Delhi-walla or Bombayite. But let's be clear. India has a lot of cool things, but accent isn't one of them. If my Inglish smells of Keralean prawn curry,[31] that's because years of life in India have twisted my tongue and vocal cords in a unique way that you seldom experience living in a world of formal,

---

30 Khoobsoorat, popularly heard in Bollywood, means beautiful in Hindi.
31 If you are a connoisseur of spicy food, you shouldn't miss the opportunity to indulge in Keralean prawn curry in this lifetime as it offers the ultimate delight to the palate. We recommend keeping a box of tissues next to you, since the curry is known to bring out copious amount of tears from the eyes.

buttoned-up Received Pronunciation speakers. When my ancestors spoke a different language for thousands of years, it's natural that my English has a different flavor from yours, no matter whether I live in Alaska or Australia.

Now don't leap to the conclusion that I am a vernacular chauvinist pig. There's no doubt English is the global language of the world, thanks to British colonialism of the 18th century and American capitalism of the 19th century. It is the third largest language in terms of native speakers, after Chinese Mandarin and Spanish, and arguably the largest among all speakers. While words of English origin appear in many languages, English itself has borrowed heavily from foreign languages, including those from the subcontinent. If you think English words like mantra, juggernaut and jodhpurs, have some Indian connections, you are not off the mark, for they are now entrenched in the English vocabulary.

For an outsider, it's natural to think Hindi as the official language of India. Indeed it is, but along with Hindi, English has also earned the title of the official language. What many people don't realize is India, with its one billion people, is the country with the second-largest number of English speakers, next only to the United States. Guess what? When more Indians start speaking English, the English language will shift from its genteel European accent to the spicy curry-flavored accent of the subcontinent that we call Inglish.

Professor David Crystal, author of the *Cambridge Encyclopedia of the English Language*, predicts Inglish will become the most widely spoken variant based on India's sheer population size and its prosperity in the global economy. "If 100 million Indians pronounce an English word in a certain way, this is more than Britain's population—so it's the only way to pronounce it. If British English was the world language at the end of the 19th century after a century of imperialism, and American English is the world language today after the American 20th century, then the language of the 21st century might well be Indian English or at least an English heavily influenced by India ..."

Just when you thought Inglish would remain confined within call centers and Bollywood, it promises to be the currency of the future in a world that is becoming increasingly smaller through the effects of globalization. When the West becomes more familiar with Inglish, dinner conversations will take place in the company of Vindaloo and Roghan

Josh, instead of baked potatoes and steak. Sexual harassment will cease to exist and be replaced by politically incorrect eve teasing, its Inglish counterpart. And when you get a taste of the history of the land that produced this mongrel language, household names like Chattopadhyay and Gopalakrishna will no longer be foot-long tongue twisters for you.

Some day in the future, beautiful Inglish words like Jodi and Tamasha will become common parlance among people of all folds. Then, my friend, you will be ready to play the game in my terms. We'll first celebrate over a plate of Tandoori chicken followed by mango Lassi. Then it will be time to indulge in dumplings and spring rolls. But that will be just starters in our quest to tame this Eastern dragon called Chinese Mandarin, spoken by over a billion people. At the present rate of population growth, India is estimated to overtake China as the world's most populous nation by 2035.

But you don't need to wait until 2035. There's no doubt Inglish is here to stay. So please stop whining about call-center calls and get used to the Indian accent ☺.

INDEX

CPSIA information can be obtained at www.ICGtesting.com
Printed in the USA
LVOW07s1729090314

376632LV00001B/454/P